CUSTOM CURRICULUM

What, Me Holy?

Fran and Jill Sciacca

Paul Woods

David C. Cook Publishing Co.
Elgin, Illinois—Weston, Ontario

Custom Curriculum
What, Me Holy?

Published by David C. Cook Publishing Co.
850 North Grove Ave., Elgin, IL 60120
Cable address: DCCOOK
Series creator: John Duckworth
Series editor: Randy Southern
Editor: Randy Southern
Option writers: Rick Thompson, Nelson E. Copeland, Jr., and Ellen Larson
Designer: Bill Paetzold
Cover illustrator: Paul Turnbaugh
Inside illustrator: Al Hering
Printed in U.S.A.

ISBN: 0-7814-5010-1

CONTENTS

About the Authors 4

You've Made the Right Choice! 5

Talking to Kids about Holiness
by Fran and Jill Sciacca 9

Publicity Clip Art 12

Sessions by Paul Woods
Options by Rick Thompson, Nelson E. Copeland, Jr., and Ellen Larson

Session One
How Can Anybody Be Holy? 14

Session Two
What's Right? What's Wrong? 30

Session Three
If Sin Is Fun, Why Stay Clean? 46

Session Four
Resisting the Wrong 62

Session Five
Fighting for Right 78

About the Authors

Paul Woods is an editor at Zondervan Publishing House and a past managing editor of Group Books. A former youth pastor, he helped create the *Pacesetter* series of youth resources for David C. Cook.

Rick Thompson is managing editor of youth and young adult products at David C. Cook. Active in youth work at his church, he is also a contributor to the *Hot Topics Youth Electives* series (Cook).

Nelson E. Copeland, Jr. is a nationally known speaker and the author of several youth resources including *Great Games for City Kids* (Youth Specialties) and *A New Agenda for Urban Youth* (Winston-Derek). He is president of the Christian Education Coalition for African-American Leadership (CECAAL), an organization dedicated to reinforcing educational and cultural excellence among urban teenagers. He also serves as youth pastor at the First Baptist Church in Morton, Pennsylvania.

Ellen Larson is an educator and writer with degrees in education and theology. She has served as minister of Christian education in several churches, teaching teens and children, as well as their teachers. Her experience also includes teaching in public schools. She is the author of several books for Christian education teachers, and frequently leads training seminars for volunteer teachers. Ellen and her husband live in San Diego and are the parents of two daughters.

You've Made the Right Choice!

Thanks for choosing **Custom Curriculum**! We think your choice says at least three things about you:

(1) You know your group pretty well, and want your program to fit that group like a glove;

(2) You like having options instead of being boxed in by some far-off curriculum editor;

(3) You have a small mole on your left forearm, exactly two inches above the elbow.

OK, so we were wrong about the mole. But if you like having choices that help you tailor meetings to fit your kids, **Custom Curriculum** *is* the best place to be.

Going through Customs

In this (and every) **Custom Curriculum** volume, you'll find

• five great sessions you can use anytime, in any order.

• reproducible student handouts, at least one per session.

• a truckload of options for adapting the sessions to your group (more about that in a minute).

• a helpful get-you-ready article by a youth expert.

• clip art for making posters, fliers, and other kinds of publicity to get kids to your meetings.

Each **Custom Curriculum** session has three to six steps. No matter how many steps a session has, it's designed to achieve these goals:

• *Getting together.* Using an icebreaker activity, you'll help kids be glad they came to the meeting.

• *Getting thirsty.* Why should kids care about your topic? Why should they care what the Bible has to say about it? You'll want to take a few minutes to earn their interest before you start pouring the "living water."

• *Getting the Word.* By exploring and discussing carefully selected passages, you'll find out what God has to say.

• *Getting the point.* Here's where you'll help kids make the leap from principles to nitty-gritty situations they are likely to face.

• *Getting personal.* What should each group member do as a result of this session? You'll help each person find a specific "next-step" response that works for him or her.

Each session is written to last 45 to 60 minutes. But what if you have less time—or more? No problem! **Custom Curriculum** is all about … options!

What Are My Options?

Every **Custom Curriculum** session gives you fourteen kinds of options:

• *Extra Action*—for groups that learn better when they're physically moving (instead of just reading, writing, and discussing).

• *Combined Junior High/High School*—to use when you're mixing age levels, and an activity or case study would be too "young" or "old" for part of the group.

• *Small Group*—for adapting activities that would be tough with groups of fewer than eight kids.

• *Large Group*—to alter steps for groups of more than twenty kids.

• *Urban*—for fitting sessions to urban facilities and multiethnic (especially African-American) concerns.

• *Heard It All Before*—for fresh approaches that get past the defenses of kids who are jaded by years in church.

• *Little Bible Background*—to use when most of your kids are strangers to the Bible, or haven't made a Christian commitment.

• *Mostly Guys*—to focus on guys' interests and to substitute activities they might be more enthused about.

• *Mostly Girls*—to address girls' concerns and to substitute activities they might prefer.

• *Extra Fun*—for longer, more "rowdy" youth meetings where the emphasis is on fun.

• *Short Meeting Time*—tips for condensing the session to 30 minutes or so.

• *Fellowship & Worship Options*—for building deeper relationships or enabling kids to praise God together.

• *Media Options*—to spice up meetings with video, music, or other popular media.

• *Sixth Grade*—appearing only in junior high/middle school volumes, this option helps you change steps that sixth graders might find hard to understand or relate to.

• *Extra Challenge*—appearing only in high school volumes, this option lets you crank up the voltage for kids who are ready for more Scripture or more demanding personal application.

Each kind of option is offered twice in each session. So in this book, you get *almost 150* ways to tweak the meetings to fit your group!

Customizing a Session

All right, you may be thinking. *With all of these options flying around, how do I put a session together? I don't have a lot of time, you know.*

We know! That's why we've made **Custom Curriculum** as easy to follow as possible. Let's take a look at how you might prepare an actual meeting. You can do that in four easy steps:

(1) *Read the basic session plan.* Start by choosing one or more of the goals listed at the beginning of the session. You have three to pick from: a goal that emphasizes *knowledge*, one that stresses *understanding*, and one that emphasizes *action*. Choose one or more, depending on what *you* want to accomplish. Then read the basic plan to see what will work for you and what might not.

(2) *Choose your options.* You don't *have* to use any options at all; the

basic session plan would work well for many groups, and you may want to stick with it if you have absolutely no time to consider options. But if you want a more perfect fit, check out your choices.

As you read the basic session plan, you'll see small symbols in the margin. Each symbol stands for a different kind of option. When you see a symbol, it means that kind of option is offered for that step. Turn to the page noted by the symbol and you'll see that option explained.

Let's say you have a small group, mostly guys who get bored if they don't keep moving. You'll want to keep an eye out for three kinds of options: Small Group, Mostly Guys, and Extra Action. As you read the basic session, you might spot symbols that tell you there are Small Group options for Step 1 and Step 3—maybe a different way to play a game so that you don't need big teams, and a way to cover several Bible passages when just a few kids are looking them up. Then you see symbols telling you that there are Mostly Guys options for Step 2 and Step 4—perhaps a substitute activity that doesn't require too much self-disclosure, and a case study guys will relate to. Finally you see symbols indicating Extra Action options for Step 2 and Step 3—maybe an active way to get kids' opinions instead of handing out a survey, and a way to act out some verses instead of just looking them up.

After reading the options, you might decide to use four of them. You base your choices on your personal tastes and the traits of your group that you think are most important right now. **Custom Curriculum** offers you more options than you'll need, so you can pick your current favorites and plug others into future meetings if you like.

(3) *Use the checklist.* Once you've picked your options, keep track of them with the simple checklist that appears at the end of each option section (just before the start of the next session plan). This little form gives you a place to write down the materials you'll need too—since they depend on the options you've chosen.

(4) *Get your stuff together.* Gather your materials; photocopy any Repro Resources (reproducible student sheets) you've decided to use. And . . . you're ready!

The Custom Curriculum Challenge

Your kids are fortunate to have you as their leader. You see them not as a bunch of generic teenagers, but as real, live, unique kids. You care whether you really connect with them. That's why you're willing to take a few extra minutes to tailor your meetings to fit.

It's a challenge to work with real, live kids, isn't it? We think you deserve a standing ovation for taking that challenge. And we pray that **Custom Curriculum** helps you shape sessions that shape lives for Jesus Christ and His kingdom.

—The Editors

Talking to Kids about Holiness

by Fran and Jill Sciacca

A world without boundaries provides a life without meaning. Today's kids are growing up in a society that is swiftly becoming an ocean without a shore. From talk in the school lunchroom to television at home, the message making waves is "Life is what you make it. Party hard. Look out only for yourself." The notion that there are standards anywhere for anything is outdated. Professional athletes regularly demonstrate disrespect for the rules of the game. Politicians disregard personal moral standards. Preachers bypass the very biblical principles they preach from the pulpit. Even parents allow marriages to dissolve under the battered banner, "Christians aren't perfect, just forgiven."

Though it's a discouraging beginning, it is essential that you are alert and able to assess who and what you will be facing before you teach. You must realize that the majority of high school kids in your group have no genuine idea or knowledge about personal holiness. And those who think they do may actually possess some residual version handed down to them without explanation by a well-meaning adult. Your task is enormous. But it is equally attainable! *What, Me Holy?* is carefully constructed to equip you to lead your group into an understanding of what holiness is, and to help you instill in them a passion to be holy. As you approach the task of teaching, remember that *you* are a student too. Approach the material with humility and a healthy desire to learn from the Lord yourself.

What Is Holiness?

Probably the greatest hindrance in understanding holiness is rooted in our confusion over the meaning of the word. Most Christians speak of it as though it were some vague or lofty concept—something far off and unobtainable. We speak of holy days, the Holy Bible, etc. But the word, when used to describe people, is really much more down to earth. It doesn't describe people or things. It simply states what we are or should be. The word *hagios,* which is translated "holy," has one primary meaning—to be different or distinct.

Holiness is not the same as righteousness. To be righteous has to do with our accepted position in the sight of God. Because of Jesus Christ's death and resurrection, we possess the very righteousness of God (II Corinthians 5:21). Accepting His forgiveness, we share His nature (II Peter 1:4). But holiness is something different. It means to be set apart. This is important because young people think of holiness first and foremost as something to attain and then maintain. Quickly it degenerates into a type of works—one more responsibility to fulfill or fail. That is wrong. Something that is holy is set apart for a purpose. As you lead these sessions, keep this distinction clear. Look for the common misunderstanding in the questions you're asked and in the statements that are made. Don't be surprised to hear "I've tried to be holy—it's too hard!"

Being Different Isn't Distasteful!

The desire to be different is definitely part of the teenage years. Teens seem to possess an innate sense that being "set apart" or different is the path to personal fulfillment. The irony, of course, is that most teens are actually carbon copies of their friends and that they have a haunting fear of being genuinely distinct from everyone else! Yet, there exists deep within them a belief that being different is cool. Use this urge to your advantage. Build on it. Draw from it. Ask about it. Make it your aim to shed spiritual light upon the shadowy desire to be set apart and distinct. You will be able to assist your young people in assembling a mental model of what "different" means from God's perspective—a perspective found in the principles of Scripture. The supreme command God has given to us is to "be holy, because [He] is holy" (I Peter 1:16). What an exciting challenge!

"Holy" Ain't Happening Much Where I Live!

One of the things I see happening in my own Christian school classrooms will probably happen to you. My students are interpreting biblical truth in light of their own homes. If the truth is too painful, they will either reject it or redefine it so that they can live with it.

One day while discussing the portion of Matthew 5 that deals with divorce and remarriage, one of my students started to softly weep. After class I asked her what was wrong. She told me she was trying to understand her parents' recent decision to call it quits in light of the difficult passage we were discussing. She did not want to believe that Scripture spoke so strongly about a subject that her parents were bypassing.

It is likely that as you pursue the issue of personal holiness, questions will come up about unholy choices parents are making, or about Christian church leaders or friends who live one life at church and another at home or at school. Make it your aim to focus on how the truth at hand touches the one *asking* the question, not someone else. Do not take the opportunity to point out an error that exists in their own home. If you force group members to take sides, they will—and you will be the enemy! Direct their personal gaze to God's Word. Then slowly let Scripture speak to their own lives, not Mom's or Dad's, not the church leaders', not their peers'. Young people tend to "go global" in their thinking and in their feelings. But in the area of holiness, it is appropriate for us to allow our teens to focus on themselves.

Holiness Is a Choice, Not a Plateau

Young people also have a tendency to project today into tomorrow. A single failure can be evidence to them that things are hopeless. If holiness is presented as a goal to reach, failure will be grounds to give up. In nearly twenty years of youth work, I have met few high school students who can find hope beyond failure. They set their standards so high—only to have them dashed before the bell rings that day. We need to help young people see that holiness is a moment-by-moment choice to be different. One failure can be followed by one success. The essential need is for you to help them define holiness as it is presented in Scripture. Them help them discover tangible, biblical ways to be different—to be like Christ.

Jill and I have four children. Our junior high-age son, Geoff, is the easiest to teach about holiness. His passion to be different is profound. He wants to wear a ponytail and an earring in a school with a strict conservative dress code. If you asked Geoff why, he would smile and say, "I just want to be different!" We can't let him beat the system, but we can carefully help Geoff see that he can be distinct from his friends in a way that has eternal value. We've discussed holiness without really using the word. Jill spends time with Geoff several days a week working slowly through Proverbs. Geoff is seeing that compassion, an absence of sarcasm, convictions about honesty, and respect for authority are traits that are really "different" in the junior high jungle. He's working hard not to retaliate when he gets verbally attacked at school. Jill holds him accountable. They assess the daily battles—both victories and defeats. Geoff is making headway on the path to personal holiness.

Holy Is the Choice of Champions

Probably the most significant thing you can accomplish as you work through this book is to link the idea of holiness with the person of Jesus Christ. For most young people, being a Christian has little to do with being like the One who saved them. But it is clearly God's desire and design that we become like His Son (Romans 8:29). In the Gospels, we have a detailed description of a man so different that people were drawn to Him wherever He went. Christ set up a counterculture that shook the world of His day—and lives on, because He lives in us.

Holiness may be a lost concept in our culture. But you have the opportunity and challenge to hold forth a fresh truth to a generation that desperately wants a definition of how to be different. You can help them see that what they once thought was distasteful is really desirable. What they once thought was unattainable isn't. The answer to the baffling question "What, me holy?" is "You bet!"

Fran and Jill Sciacca have been involved with youth ministry for nearly two decades. Fran is a graduate of Denver Seminary. He has been teaching high school Bible since 1980 in a large Christian school serving students from over 180 local churches. Jill has a degree in journalism and sociology and is a full-time homemaker and free-lance writer/editor. She has written for Discipleship Journal *and* Decision *magazine, and has served on the editorial team for the* Youth Bible *(Word, Inc.). Fran and Jill coauthored* Lifelines *(Zondervan), an award-winning Bible study series for high schoolers. Fran is the author of the best-selling Bible study,* To Walk and Not Grow Weary *(NavPress), as well as* Generation at Risk *(Moody), and* Wounded Saints *(Baker). Fran and Jill have four children—two daughters and two sons. The Sciaccas live in Colorado Springs.*

Publicity Clip Art

The images on these two pages are designed to help you promote this course within your church and community. Feel free to photocopy anything here and adapt it to fit your publicity needs. The stuff on this page could be used as a flier that you send or hand out to kids—or as a bulletin insert. The stuff on the next page could be used to add visual interest to newsletters, calendars, bulletin boards, or other promotions. Be creative and have fun!

If Sin Is Fun, Why Stay Clean?

When God calls us to be holy, is He asking us to stop having fun? What does it mean to be holy, anyway? Is it really possible to be holy and still be normal? How can we fight temptation when it's so much easier to give in? Come and get the answers you need when we start a new series called *What, Me Holy?*

Who:

When:

Where:

Questions? Call:

What, Me Holy?

What, Me Holy?

Come and see what's cooking!

Don't put it off.

How can you tell
right from wrong?

(Write your own message on the screen.)

SESSION

1

How Can Anybody Be Holy?

YOUR GOALS FOR THIS SESSION:

Choose one or more

- [ ] To help kids recognize what holiness is and isn't.
- [ ] To help kids understand that being holy doesn't mean being "weird."
- [ ] To help kids determine to work toward pleasing God in their lives.
- [ ] Other ______________________________

Your Bible Base:

Psalm 99
Colossians 3:1-17

STEP 1

Perfection

(Needed: Copies of Repro Resource 1, pencils, pennies, nickels, dimes, quarters)

OPTIONS

Distribute copies of "Picture Perfect" (Repro Resource 1) and pencils. Give group members a few minutes to complete the sheet. When everyone is finished, quickly judge each sheet by placing a penny, nickel, dime, or quarter over each circle. Select one person's paper as the most "perfect" one. It will speed things up if you have several coins available and have kids "grade" each other's attempts. Congratulate your winner by announcing that his or her drawing was most *nearly* perfect. But quickly add that since it wasn't *exactly* perfect, no one will get a prize.

Ask: **Why can't we say that anyone did a perfect job on this?** (Because it was just too difficult; people can't be that steady and accurate, especially when drawing with their eyes closed or with their mouth.)

Is it possible for anyone to be perfect at anything? (Some bowlers bowl perfect games, some golfers get a hole in one, some gymnasts score perfect marks—but none of them do it all the time.) Ask for other examples of "perfection," outside the sports world.

Summarize: **Perfection is pretty tough to attain. In fact, it's impossible to attain in most things. But that doesn't mean we shouldn't always keep trying to do better.**

STEP 2

One Perfect Person

(Needed: Chalkboard and chalk or newsprint and marker)

Say: **Since we're talking about perfection, what do you think it would mean to be spiritually perfect?** (Never committing a sin, depending on God all the time, always helping and encouraging others, knowing the Bible well enough to quote relevant verses whenever necessary, etc.) Encourage several group members to offer their ideas. Write the ideas on the board as they are named.

After you've received several ideas, ask: **Besides Jesus, can anybody be spiritually perfect? Why or why not?** (Some group members may say that, because we've sinned, we can never be totally perfect. Others may say that though we've messed up in the past, we can be perfect with God's help.) If you get differing opinions, encourage some debate on the matter.

Then say: **Jesus was the only person who was able to be completely perfect spiritually throughout His entire life. The Bible tells us He never sinned. Perfection may not be possible for us, but we can still live lives that are pleasing to God.**

Some people talk about being "holy." What does that mean? (Some group members may say that it means to be really spiritual. Others may say that it means to always obey God. Some may think that it means being spiritually perfect. They may view holiness as something unobtainable.) Encourage several group members to offer their suggestions.

Then say: **Let's see what the Bible says about what it means to be holy.**

[NOTE: Holiness is a difficult concept to grasp and is often misunderstood. The danger you need to avoid is giving the impression that what we do or don't do determines how holy we are. We are holy because God sets us apart to serve Him. It's much more than a bunch of dos and don'ts. Yet, what we do is a direct reflection of our desire to lead holy lives. When we realize we are holy and dearly loved by God, our actions and attitudes will come to reflect this. This course will deal with some of these "reflections." Today's session focuses on what holiness is. The next session focuses on our ability to choose between right and wrong. The following two sessions discuss temptation—*why* to resist it and *how* to resist it. The final session addresses our need to actively fight injustice. As you go through these sessions, keep in mind that your young people are still in process. Don't expect them all to live completely holy lives from this day forth. Rather, view yourself as a guide in helping them decide for themselves how to move in the right direction toward greater holiness.]

OPTIONS

LARGE GROUP

HEARD IT ALL BEFORE

LITTLE BIBLE BACKGROUND

URBAN

EXTRA CHALLENGE

STEP 3

Things Above

(Needed: Bibles, copies of Repro Resource 2, pencils)

OPTIONS

- SMALL GROUP
- LITTLE BIBLE BACKGROUND
- MEDIA
- JR. HIGH HIGH SCHOOL COMBINED
- EXTRA CHALLENGE

Explain: **When we talk about being holy, we're really talking about living our lives in ways that are pleasing to God.**

Have your group members form teams of three. Distribute copies of "On the Right Track" (Repro Resource 2) and pencils. Instruct the teams to read through Colossians 3:1-17 and answer the questions on the resource sheet.

Give the teams several minutes to work. When they're finished, go through the questions one at a time. Have each team share its response to each question. If teams come up with different responses, talk about those differences and try to reach a consensus as a group.

Use the following information to supplement the teams' responses.

(1) As Christians, what should we be concentrating on? (Things above, and not earthly things.)

What does that mean? (We should think about what God wants us to do. We shouldn't worry about everyday problems and situations here on earth.)

Why should we do that? (When we become Christians, every part of our lives changes—including our priorities and the things we think about. So rather than focusing our thoughts on earthly things as we used to do before Christ saved us, we now focus on heavenly ways of thinking about life, since heaven is where we'll be spending eternity.)

(2) As Christians, what kinds of things should we avoid? (Sexual immorality, impurity, lust, evil desires, greed, anger, rage, malice, slander, filthy language, lying.)

If we were to update this list for today's society, what kinds of things would be on it? (Among the things an updated list might tell us to avoid are premarital sex, swearing, putting others down, telling dirty jokes, gossiping, cheating in school, etc.)

Why should we avoid these things? (Our old selves—the ones for whom these types of actions would have been normal—died with Christ. In Christ, we are new and different. We are no longer controlled by our sinful nature. With God's help, we have the ability to rid our lives of these actions.)

(3) As Christians, what kinds of attitudes should be evident in our lives? (Compassion, kindness, humility, gentleness, patience, forgiveness, love, peace, thankfulness.)

How could we demonstrate these attitudes in our lives today? (Being nice to the not-so-popular kids at school, not bragging, being patient with our siblings, forgiving people who put us down, etc.)

Why should these attitudes be evident in our lives? (Because we're God's people; because we're trying to be holy; because we're thankful for all that God has done for us.)

(4) With what attitude should we approach everything we do? (With thankfulness to God and the desire to do our best for Him.)

How could we incorporate this attitude into our lives? (We could stop to think about what would please God when we have a decision to make. We could avoid things that we know would make Him sad or angry.)

Why should we have this attitude? (Because God has forgiven us; because He sent His Son to die for us; because we love Him.)

After going through all the questions on the sheet, ask: **How would you define holiness now?** (Living the best lives we can to please God; serving Him out of gratitude for what He's done for us.) Avoid giving the impression that holiness is simply based on a long list of dos and don'ts. It's much more than that. It's living life with God's perspective in mind.

On a scale of 1 to 10, with 1 being "very easy" and 10 being "nearly impossible," how easy would you say it is to be holy? Encourage several group members to offer their opinions.

STEP 4

Holy Joe

(Needed: Bibles, chalkboard and chalk or newsprint and markers)

Emphasize that holiness comes from inside—it is not the result of superficial actions and posturing. Draw two large human outlines on the board. Label one of the outlines "Externally Holy Joe" and the other one "Internally Holy Joe."

Distribute markers or pieces of chalk to your group members. Instruct them to come to the board one at a time and draw or write on each outline one way "Externally Holy Joe" might try to prove his holiness to others and one way "Internally Holy Joe" might truly demonstrate holiness in his life. Have group members refer to Colossians 3:1-17 for ideas if they have trouble.

For example, on the "Externally Holy Joe" outline, group members might draw an enormous Bible in his hand and write "Carries a big Bible

to school all the time" next to it. Or they might draw pieces of paper in his hand and write "Passes out tracts to everyone he sees" next to it. Or they might draw a halo above his head and write "Tries to make people think he's ten times as spiritual as they are" next to it.

On the "Internally Holy Joe" outline, group members might draw a large heart on his chest and write "Shows others that he really cares about them" next to it. Or they might draw a serving tray in his hand and write "Has a servant attitude" next to it. Or they might draw a smile on his face and write "Forgives people who make fun of his faith" next to it.

When group members have all had a chance to write or draw something on both human outlines, read off what they've written. Use these answers as a basis for discussion of what it really means to be holy. Make sure group members realize that being holy doesn't mean being a social weirdo, but that it usually does mean being different in some ways.

Ask: **How do some Christians turn others off toward Christianity by being different in wrong ways?** (By wearing weird clothes, never doing anything fun, always being serious, "preaching" all the time, etc.)

What are some appropriate ways for Christians to be different from non-Christians? (Christians shouldn't be stuck-up. We should always be honest. We should stay away from drugs, drunkenness, and inappropriate sexual behavior.)

Say: **These are all good ideas. But it isn't usually as easy to do these things we're talking about as it is to talk about them. Being holy involves both resisting the temptation of wrong things and being willing to do right things.**

STEP 5

Spiritual Support

(Needed: Bibles, songbooks [optional])

Have group members form teams of three or four. Instruct each team to read Colossians 3:16. Then say: **God has given us each other as support for one another in choosing to do what's right. What does this verse suggest we can do for each other?** (Encourage each other, help each other learn what's right, worship God together.)

Say: **In your teams, tell each other about one area you'd like to work on in becoming more holy. As each person shares, each of you support that person with a few words of encouragement.**

When the teams are finished, encourage them to pray together. Say: **God has also given us the Holy Spirit, who lives in us and helps us make good decisions. God sometimes uses a combination of the Holy Spirit and the Bible to remind us of what pleases Him and of how He's always there to help us when we need Him.**

If possible, wrap up your session by having your group members sing an encouraging song together. A Scripture song, such as "I Will Call upon the Lord," "I Will Enter His Gates," or "By My Spirit," would be especially appropriate. If you have songbooks with these songs in them, distribute them among your group members. If your group isn't musical, or if you don't have accompaniment available, you might want to read aloud Psalm 99 as a closing benediction. This psalm focuses on God's holiness.

OPTIONS

Picture Perfect

Complete the following instructions as quickly *and perfectly* as possible. Do not look at any coins as you do this.

1. Draw a perfect circle the size of a penny.

2. Using your other hand, draw a perfect circle the size of a nickel.

3. Using either hand, but with your eyes closed, draw a perfect circle the size of a dime.

4. Holding your pencil or pen in your mouth, draw a perfect circle the size of a quarter.

ON THE Right TRACK

Read Colossians 3:1-17. Then answer each of the following questions, based on what you discover in the passage.

1. As Christians, what should we be concentrating on?

   What does that mean?

   Why should we do that?

2. As Christians, what kinds of things should we avoid?

   If we were to update this list for today's society, what kinds of things would be on it?

   Why should we avoid these things?

3. As Christians, what kinds of attitudes should be evident in our lives?

   How could we demonstrate these attitudes in our lives today?

   Why should these attitudes be evident in our lives?

4. With what attitude should we approach everything we do?

   How could we incorporate this attitude into our lives?

   Why should we have this attitude?

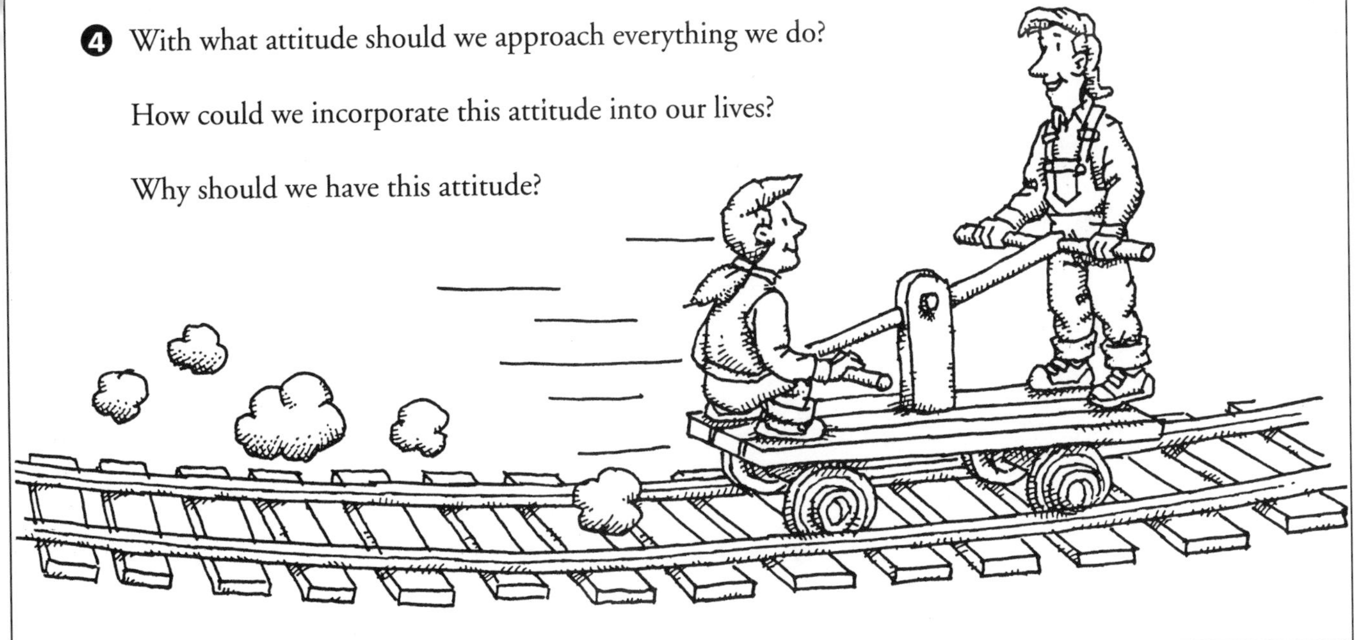

EXTRA ACTION

Step 1
Instead of using Repro Resource 1, demonstrate imperfection another way. Have group members form two teams. Explain: **We're going to begin this session with a kicking contest. Our goal is to find the perfect soccer player.**

Set up two goals at least twenty feet apart, using two chairs placed about three feet apart for each goal. Have each team line up beside one of the goals. Place a foam ball on the floor in front of one of the teams. The first person in line for that team will attempt to kick the ball through the opposite goal. However, he or she may not move any closer to the goal to kick. After that person has kicked, give the ball to the first person in line for the other team, and have him or her kick. Continue alternating between teams until all group members have had a chance to kick. Eliminate those who miss.

Then move the chairs to about two feet apart and have all remaining team members kick again. Be sure they stay at least ten to fifteen feet from the goal they're kicking toward.

Move the chairs to one foot apart for the third round.

For the fourth round, move the chairs so close together that the ball will barely fit between them. If someone happens to kick the ball through the goal in this fourth round, have that person keep kicking until he or she misses.

After the fourth round, have group members return to their seats to discuss whether perfection is possible.

Step 4
Instead of writing or drawing on outlines of Holy Joe, divide into two teams. Team 1 will develop a short skit about Externally Holy Joe at a party. One team member should act out Externally Holy Joe's part and another should speak his real thoughts out loud. The other team will develop a similar skit about Internally Holy Joe.

SMALL GROUP

Step 3
If you don't have enough group members to form teams of three, stay together as one group and work through Repro Resource 2 together. Try to get each group member involved in coming up with answers. One way to encourage this would be to have kids take turns writing down responses on the board. You start by writing down one response, then pass the marker (or chalk) to someone else. That person must then write down the next response. If he or she can't come up with anything, then it's his or her job to get others talking.

Step 5
Stay together as one group. Give everyone paper and a pencil. (Use the back side of one of the Repro Resources if you handed any out earlier.) Have each group member look over Colossians 3:1-17 and write down one verse, or a part of a verse, that convicts him or her most right now. Then, have each person make two columns, one labeled "more" and the other "less." Encourage kids to write one or more words or phrases in each column that they need to be doing in response to what they feel God is telling them to do. For example, they might be feeling like they should show more forgiveness and less anger. Allow kids to share what they've written to the extent they are comfortable. When closing in prayer, focus some attention on each group member.

LARGE GROUP

Step 2
This discussion of perfection can be made more effective in a large group by getting group members more involved. To do this, have group members form teams of four or five. Have each team compile a list of the "top ten qualities of a spiritually perfect person." Encourage humor and creativity as the teams develop their lists. Have one representative from each team share its list. Note similarities and differences. Take some time discussing how Jesus measures up against these lists, since He was spiritually perfect. Perhaps the lists reflect qualities that don't really measure spiritual perfection after all.

Step 4
In a large group setting, the activity in which kids write or draw on the outlines of Externally Holy Joe and Internally Holy Joe will work better if you break into teams and have each team complete the activity. A fun way to get the activity started would be to have the teams trace two of their own members' outlines on large sheets of paper. When each team is finished drawing/writing on its two outlines, display the outlines and have kids look them over. Have kids question one another if there are parts that don't make sense on the outlines. Ask: **Why do some people try so hard to appear holy on the outside?** (To impress others, to try to earn points with God, to cover up internal problems, etc.)

Step 2
We keep hearing that Jesus was sinless. How do we know this? Give your group five to ten minutes to "prove" that Jesus was sinless. Don't give them any Scripture references to look up. Let them find things on their own. You might want to have a concordance on hand. For your own benefit, here are a few references: Hebrews 4:15; 7:26; II Corinthians 5:21; I Peter 2:22, 24; I John 3:5. After hearing from your group, ask an even more important question: **OK, so we've established from the Bible that Jesus was sinless; what difference does that make to us today?** Help kids see how essential it was that Jesus be the perfect sacrifice for our sins. Following in His footsteps is the key to our own holiness.

Step 4
After discussing Holy Joe, have your group members read the parable of the Pharisee and the tax collector (Luke 18:9-14). Ask them how this parable relates to the two Holy Joes. Obviously, the Pharisee is acting like an Externally Holy Joe, and the tax collector is more like Internally Holy Joe. Have your group members develop a modern-day skit that parallels this parable. If you have more than one group preparing a skit, assign each group a different location—a party, a school lunchroom, church, etc.—for its skit to take place in.

Step 2
Refer to the "Heard It All Before" option for Step 2 for some Scripture verses about Jesus' sinlessness. Go through these verses and point out the importance of Jesus' sinlessness to His overall ministry and God's plan of redemption. Also summarize Romans 3:9-26—especially verse 23. Those with little Bible background may not be very familiar with the concept of sin. Without a proper understanding of sin, a discussion of holiness won't mean very much!

Step 3
The Colossians 3:1-17 passage may be a bit overwhelming to someone with little Bible background. To simplify it, you might want to make two lists on the board: dos and don'ts. Then go through the passage and put things under the two headings. While it's true that being holy is much more than following a list of dos and don'ts, what we do and don't do ultimately reflects the sincerity of our relationship with God. Ask: **How do you feel about this list? Does it seem reasonable, or is God asking too much of us? Which items on the list, in either category, do you think most people have the hardest time following? Why?** Quote Matthew 19:26 with reference to the impossibility of saving ourselves, but observing that all things are possible with God. The same is true of holiness. We can't be holy by our own efforts, but only through God's work in our lives.

Step 4
After discussing Holy Joe, have each group member complete the following sentence: "It's hardest for me to be holy when . . ." If your group is small, encourage kids to share their sentences out loud. If that's too threatening, break into teams of three for sharing. If your group is very quiet, you might want kids to write down their responses and only have a few volunteers (including you) share what they've written.

Step 5
Colossians 3:16 talks about singing psalms, hymns, and spiritual songs. With a supply of Bibles, hymnals, and chorus books, have your kids locate at least one psalm, hymn, and spiritual song that talks about the holiness of God. Review the words of each one. Here are a few psalms to get you started: Psalm 11, 24, 77, and 99. "Holy, Holy, Holy" is an obvious hymn choice. Can your kids locate another one? "Holy, Holy" (by Jimmy and Carol Owens) would be a fitting chorus. If you want, sing some of the hymns and choruses you come up with, or simply study the words. Dig deeper into what it means when we call God holy. How do your kids feel about His holiness? How should we react to it? What are some ways we sometimes take His holiness too lightly?

MOSTLY GIRLS

Step 1
If you don't think your group members will enjoy drawing circles, try the following activity. Attach a large piece of paper to the wall. Across the top of the paper, write "My Idea of Perfection Is . . ." Have your group members write their responses to the statement, covering the paper with their unsigned comments. Group members may use both serious and humorous statements for their responses. Conclude Step 1 by reading some or all of the responses aloud. Ask: **Can any of these ideas of perfection be achieved in this life? If so, how? If not, why not? Should we give up trying to be perfect? Explain.**

Step 4
To illustrate the difference between "Externally Holy Joe" and "Internally Holy Joe," ask your group members to plan and present some skits featuring each character. Have your group members form teams of three or four. Instruct half of the teams to come up with a skit featuring "Externally Holy Joe"; instruct the other half to come up with a skit featuring "Internally Holy Joe." Give the teams a few minutes to prepare; then have them present their skits.

MOSTLY GUYS

Step 4
When discussing whether it's possible to be holy without being weird, give your group the following true-false test:
1. If you're going to be holy, people are going to think you're weird.
2. It's harder for guys to be holy than it is for girls.
3. It's harder to be holy today than it was when our grandparents were young.
4. It's harder for a teenager to be holy than it is for someone who's older.
5. If you act too holy, people aren't going to want to hang around with you.
6. God doesn't expect us to be perfect, just forgiven.

Step 5
Many guys will have difficulty with such a "touchy-feely" ending to this session. Another way to wrap it up would be to discuss how guys can apply the principles found in Colossians 3:1-17 in the following situations:
• Competitive sports
• Individual sports
• Dating relationships
• Friendships
• At home (especially getting along with parents)
• At school (with teachers)
• At work (with coworkers and employers)

Ask: **What would it mean to be holy in each of these areas?** Ask for specific examples. To close, have each guy share one place where he has the most difficulty being holy.

EXTRA FUN

Step 1
Develop a "bowling" theme for the session. Set up some plastic pins (or use empty two-liter bottles) and spend some time bowling. Use a small rubber ball, or any other type of ball you have on hand. You might even want to try using a football! Talk about the difficulty of bowling a perfect game, and the impossibility of bowling a perfect game every game. You could even slip in the following "joke." Say: **I once knew a guy who bowled a three hundred and won.** When kids say that's impossible since a perfect game is 300, say: **Have you ever heard of someone who bowled a three hundred and lost?** If you go with the bowling theme, you can skip using Repro Resource 1.

Step 5
If you developed the bowling theme suggested in the "Extra Fun" option for Step 1, continue with an actual team tournament. Award prizes to the winning team(s). Serve a variety of "hole-y" foods like Ritz crackers and Swiss cheese, round pretzels, and doughnuts. See if anyone makes the connection. If the bowling idea doesn't work for you and you want to be a bit more "highbrow," you could end the session with a hole-in-one contest. Set up some sort of indoor miniature golf contest. Make the course difficult enough that no one will be able to get a perfect score.

MEDIA

Step 3

At the conclusion of this step, instead of asking kids to rate how easy it is to be holy on a scale from 1 to 10, have each kid punch in his or her number on a calculator. Push the addition sign between each entry. Divide the total by the number of kids in your group to get an average score. If there's time, you might want to consider asking a series of 1 to 10 questions along a similar line:

- **On a scale of 1 to 10—with 1 being "not holy" and 10 being "very holy"—how holy do you think most people in ministry are?**
- **What about most adults?**
- **What about you?**
- **How "cool" is it to be holy at school—with 1 being "completely uncool" and 10 being "totally cool"?**

If a calculator is too low-tech for you, the same thing could be accomplished with a personal computer and a little spreadsheet know-how.

Step 4

Cut out pictures of various people from magazines and have kids rate them on how holy they think each person is. (You could use a scale of 1 to 10 like in the "Media" option for Step 3.) Try to get a wide variety of pictures—some of famous people, some of ordinary people. Ask: **On what criteria are we basing our evaluations? What danger is there in judging how holy people are by how they look or what they do? In what ways can a person's looks, style of dress, or actions demonstrate his or her internal holiness?**

SHORT MEETING TIME

Step 1

Instead of giving everyone a copy of Repro Resource 1, select three or four volunteers to compete in a perfect circle competition. Have them attempt to draw perfect circles the size of various objects (a paper plate, a Pepsi or Coke can, etc.) on the board. The rest of the group can judge who came closest, but should be very critical in finding imperfections, even among the best circles. If you're very short on time, have your group try to hum a tune in perfect harmony—while holding their noses. It can't be done! Use this to lead into a discussion of how difficult total perfection is—especially spiritual perfection.

Step 4

Drawing and writing on the Holy Joe outlines might take more time than you have. If this is the case, simply discuss the differences between internal and external holiness. Ask for specific examples for each option. Spend a little time talking about Jesus and what His life teaches us about holiness. Ask: **What were some of the outward signs that He had internal holiness?** (Examples might include showing compassion, spending time in prayer with the Father, getting angry about injustice and greed, etc.)

URBAN

Step 1

If you'd like a more active opener than Repro Resource 1, but don't have enough room in your meeting area for the soccer activity suggested in the "Extra Action" option for Step 1, try a game of "trash basketball" instead. Put two trash cans on opposite sides of the room. Have group members form two teams. Give each team a supply of wadded paper. Team members will take turns shooting baskets. If a person misses a shot, he or she is out. When all of the members of one team are out, award prizes to the other team. Then have the remaining contestants continue shooting until all of them miss a shot. Afterward, discuss as a group whether perfection—in trash basketball or any other area of life—is possible.

Step 2

Be sure to give your group members an accurate understanding of spiritual perfection. Some of your teens may assume that spiritual perfection—or even pleasing God—is impossible to pursue because they've already "messed up." Explain: **Spiritual perfection, or striving to please God, is not necessarily a matter of keeping a bunch of rules. It's more a matter of trying to be more and more like Jesus each day. One mistake doesn't eliminate us from God's favor. He allows us start again fresh each time we mess up—if we just ask for His forgiveness.** Emphasize that striving to please God should be a day-to-day activity.

JR. HIGH / HIGH SCHOOL COMBINED

Step 3
Repro Resource 2 may be too involved for most junior highers. If you don't think it will work for your group, skip it and try another option. Label two columns on the board. Column 1 should say "Earthly Things," and Column 2 should say "Things Above." Break into teams (or stay together in one group if you have five or fewer kids). Have each team make lists of items from the Colossians 3:1-17 passage that would fall into each category. After the teams share their lists, ask: **What do these lists have to do with being holy?**

Step 5
Some junior highers will be uncomfortable with, if not incapable of, sharing at the level called for in this step. A less threatening way to get some of this same information would be to have each group member select one word (or short phrase) from the Colossians 3:1-17 text that he or she needs to work on in order to be more holy. Examples might include negative words like greed, anger, bad language, and lies; or positive words like humility, love, and unity. Give each person a supply of square Post-It notes, or other small squares of paper. Have kids write one letter of the word they've chosen on each square. See if the entire group can combine all the words in crossword form on the floor or on a table. Allow kids to say why they chose the word they did as they are attempting to fit their words together.

EXTRA CHALLENGE

Step 2
When discussing whether spiritual perfection is possible, have group members look up Matthew 5:48, which tells us to be perfect as our heavenly Father is perfect. Then have them look up I Peter 1:13-16, which tells us to be holy just as God is holy. Ask: **What's the connection between these two passages? What's the connection between perfection and holiness? Do you think it's possible to be perfect or be as holy as God? Why or why not? Why would these passages be included in our Bibles if it weren't possible to follow them completely? Looking at the verses surrounding Matthew 5:48, what type of perfection do you think Jesus is talking about? How would you define holiness from the I Peter passage?** (This question provides a nice transition into Step 3.)

Step 3
When discussing the Colossians 3:1-17 passage, don't settle for any pat answers. You may want to supplement the questions in the session with the following questions as needed: **Is there a difference between setting our hearts on something** (vs. 1) **and setting our minds on something** (vs. 2)**? Does this mean we shouldn't concern ourselves with sports, current events, etc.? In order to avoid the things mentioned in this passage, should Christians not watch TV or go to movies? Does this mean we should avoid people who do these things? Is it possible to associate with unholy people or things and still be holy? In what sense are we God's chosen people? How does someone clothe himself or herself with the things mentioned in verse 12? What does it mean to do something in the name of Jesus? Are we supposed to give thanks for bad things that happen to people?**

PLANNING CHECKLIST

Date Used:

Approx. Time

Step 1: Perfection _____
o Extra Action
o Mostly Girls
o Extra Fun
o Short Meeting Time
o Urban
Things needed:

Step 2: One Perfect Person _____
o Large Group
o Heard It All Before
o Little Bible Background
o Urban
o Extra Challenge
Things needed:

Step 3: Things Above _____
o Small Group
o Little Bible Background
o Media
o Combined Junior High/High School
o Extra Challenge
Things needed:

Step 4: Holy Joe _____
o Extra Action
o Large Group
o Heard It All Before
o Fellowship & Worship
o Mostly Girls
o Mostly Guys
o Media
o Short Meeting Time
Things needed:

Step 5: Spiritual Support _____
o Small Group
o Fellowship & Worship
o Mostly Guys
o Extra Fun
o Combined Junior High/High School
Things needed:

SESSION

2 What's Right? What's Wrong?

YOUR GOALS FOR THIS SESSION:

Choose one or more

- ☐ To help kids grapple with the difficulty of determining right and wrong and see how this relates to being holy.
- ☐ To help kids understand that right and wrong actions can usually be determined by identifying who we are trying to please with our actions.
- ☐ To help kids determine to eliminate wrong attitudes and actions from their lives and exhibit right ones.
- ☐ Other ______________________________

Your Bible Base:

Galatians 5:16-26

STEP
I

Spelling Bee Real

(Needed: Copies of Repro Resource 3, pencils, small prize [optional])

OPTIONS

Hand out copies of "Right or Wrong?" (Repro Resource 3) and pencils. You'll probably get some groans when group members figure out that this is a spelling quiz. Working individually, have group members cross off all the misspelled words on the page. It's a bit tricky, because four of the words in the introduction are wrong—but don't tell anyone this—let kids figure it out for themselves. The four wrong words in the introduction are: passtime, inteligent, recieving, and mispelled. The other wrong words on the page are as follows:

(1) B (ambulence)
(2) B (embarass)
(3) A (beatle)
(4) A (wierd)
(5) B (irrelevent)
(6) B (dachshound)
(7) A (irresistable)
(8) A (sargeant)
(9) A (hippotimus)
(10) B (bizzare)
(11) A (seperate)
(12) B (priviledge)

Award a small prize to your best speller, if you want.

Then ask: **How is this test a bit like telling right from wrong in other areas of life?** (Sometimes things appear right when they are in fact wrong. Sometimes the differences are very subtle. Sometimes we've been led to believe something is right, even though it isn't.)

How do we determine whether an action is good or bad, right or wrong? (If something helps another person, pleases God, or is selfless, it is usually considered good or right. If something is against the law, hurts another person, or goes against the Bible, it's bad or wrong.)

How could we find out the proper spelling of the words on this sheet? (Use a dictionary or a spell-checker, ask a good speller, etc. Some might know the correct spelling from previous study.)

What resources do we have to help us decide whether our choices and actions are right or wrong? (The Bible, the Holy Spirit, our consciences, the opinions of Christians we respect and trust, etc.)

Explain: **Even with all of these resources available to us, it's still not always easy to tell what's right and what's wrong, especially in some of life's gray areas. Making wise moral choices is a lot more complex than simply spelling things correctly. In this session, we're going to talk more about how we can tell the difference between right and wrong.**

STEP

2

Who's Been Bad or Good?

(Needed: At least one cut-apart copy of Repro Resource 4, chalkboard and chalk or newsprint and marker)

Before the session, you'll need to cut apart at least one copy of "Wrongdoers" (Repro Resource 4). If you have more than eight group members, make extra copies so that each person can have at least two slips.

Distribute two slips from the resource sheet to each group member. Instruct group members to find someone in the group who's done what's listed on their slips and get that person to initial the slip of paper. When a group member finds one of the people he or she is looking for, the two should briefly discuss whether the action was right or wrong. Then they should move on to find the next person.

Give group members a few minutes to complete the assignment. Then bring them back together as a group.

Go over the actions listed on the slips one at a time and, without any discussion, have group members vote as to whether they think each action is right or wrong. Write on the board any actions that get votes for being both right and wrong.

If there seems to be some disagreement over any of the items, say: **We appear to disagree on some of these issues. Maybe that's OK—but maybe it's not.**

Is it possible that some things are right for some people and not right for others? Explain. (Some group members may say no, because God has the same standard for everyone. Others may say yes, because people feel differently about certain moral issues. Others may point out that the rightness or wrongness of an action depends on the circumstances.)

Say: **We're not going to make a judgment on this question. But we are going to take a look at some principles from**

O P T I O N S

Scripture that may help us make some decisions about right and wrong.

STEP 3

Who Are We Trying to Please?

(Needed: Bibles, paper, pencils)

OPTIONS

Say: **One way the Bible distinguishes between right and wrong is by identifying who we are trying to please with our actions. If we're trying to please our sinful human nature, we'll do wrong things. If we're trying to please the Holy Spirit living in us, we'll do right things. The choices we make in our daily lives is an indication of whether or not we are living in a holy way.**

Have someone read aloud Galatians 5:16-18. Then say: **These verses describe two different ways of living. What's the difference between them?** (Living by the Spirit and living by sinful human nature involves different desires.)

The next few verses in this passage go on to detail some things that are definitely right and definitely wrong. We're going to take a closer look at these verses.

Have group members form two teams. Distribute paper and pencils to each team. Instruct one team to read Galatians 5:19-21; instruct the other team to read Galatians 5:22-26.

Explain: **In your assigned passage, you will find a list of actions and attitudes. For those of you looking at verses 19-21, this list will be of negative things—actions and attitudes that are wrong. For those of you looking at verses 22-26, the list will be of positive things—actions and attitudes that are right.**

Your assignment is to come up with a modern example for each action or attitude on your list. For instance, in verse 20, "fits of rage" is listed. A modern example of a fit of rage might be child abuse or a drive-by gang shooting.

Give the teams several minutes to work. When they're finished, read aloud Galatians 5:19-21. Then have the team that was assigned that passage share its responses. Encourage members of the other team to respond to any examples they don't think are accurate. If there is a debate, discuss the matter and try to reach a consensus, if at all possible.

Then read aloud Galatians 5:22-26. Have the team that was assigned that passage share its responses. Again, encourage members of the other team to respond to any examples they don't think are accurate.

Explain: **This passage from Galatians can be helpful to us in determining what's right and what's wrong. Not only does it list specific rights and wrongs, it also gives us principles that we can apply to any "questionable" areas.**

What is the key principle in this passage that we should keep in mind for determining right and wrong? (If an action is done to satisfy the Holy Spirit, it is right. If an action is done to satisfy our sinful human nature, it is wrong.)

Say: **This principle may help us make some decisions on those actions we weren't sure about earlier.**

STEP
4

Another Look

(Needed: Chalkboard and chalk or newsprint and marker, Bibles)

Refer to the list of "questionable" actions (the actions on Repro Resource 4 that received both "right" and "wrong" votes from your group members) you wrote on the board in Step 2. If there wasn't any disagreement on these items, have your group go through some of the items, stating under what circumstances some of them would be right. Discuss these items, using the following questions. Have group members look back at Galatians 5:16-26 for guidance.

Would this action be done to satisfy the Holy Spirit or the sinful human nature?

How would doing this action affect our walk with God?

When you've finished with the list, have group members try to stump each other by coming up with difficult situations in which to decide right and wrong. Use the previous two questions to help group members decide. Try to come to agreement on what's right and what's not.

If your group members have trouble agreeing on some, say: **Not all Christians agree on what is satisfying to the Spirit and what is satisfying to the sinful nature. Therefore, we have disagreements on specific actions. When that happens, we have to study Scripture for ourselves, ask for God's guidance, and make our own decisions.**

OPTIONS

SMALL GROUP

MOSTLY GIRLS

JR. HIGH HIGH SCHOOL COMBINED

STEP
5

By His Spirit

(Needed: Chalkboard and chalk or newsprint and marker, Bibles)

Say: **Because our attitudes tend to dictate our actions, let's think a minute about what attitudes tend to produce the kinds of actions we want in our lives.**

On the board, create two columns. Label one column "By the Spirit" and the other "Not by the Spirit." Have group members call out attitudes to list under each one. Don't quit until you have at least five attitudes listed under each category. Encourage kids to think of actions beyond those listed in the verses.

"By the Spirit" attitudes might include patience, kindness, concern for others, humility, self-control, and thankfulness. "Not by the Spirit" attitudes might include selfishness, jealousy, sexual immorality, backbiting, and hatred.

Have group members form pairs. Read aloud Galatians 5:24-26. Then say: **Maintaining Spirit-led attitudes in our lives will help us keep our actions in line. Take a good look at this chart. Think about the attitudes that you exhibit most often. Share with your partner at least one negative attitude you want to work on eliminating in your life, and one positive attitude you want to work on exhibiting more.**

Give the pairs about two minutes to share; then have them pray with and for each other (if you don't think they'll be too uncomfortable doing that). Close the session by praying aloud that your group members will follow through on their commitments.

Right or Wrong?

Spelling probably isn't your favorite passtime, but we're trying to make a point about the difficulty of telling right from wrong. Don't worry, this isn't a test of how inteligent you are—and you won't be recieving a grade. Simply cross off all the mispelled words on this page.

A	B
1. *Ambulance*	*Ambulence*
2. Embarrass	**Embarass**
3. Beatle	*Beetle*
4. Wierd	**Weird**
5. Irrelevant	**Irrelevent**

A	B
6. Dachshund	*Dachshound*
7. Irresistable	Irresistible
8. SARGEANT	**SERGEANT**
9. Hippopotimus	Hippopotamus
10. Bizarre	**Bizzare**
11. Seperate	***Separate***
12. Privilege	Priviledge

WRONGDOERS

1. FIND SOMEONE WHO HAS DRIVEN AT LEAST TEN MILES PER HOUR OVER THE SPEED LIMIT.

2. FIND SOMEONE WHO HAS CUT IN LINE.

3. FIND SOMEONE WHO HAS COPIED SOMEONE ELSE'S HOMEWORK.

4. FIND SOMEONE WHO HAS TASTED BEER.

5. FIND SOMEONE WHO HAS MADE A COPY OF SOMEONE ELSE'S CASSETTE TAPE OR CD.

6. FIND SOMEONE WHO HAS FLIRTED WITH HIS OR HER BEST FRIEND'S GIRLFRIEND OR BOYFRIEND.

7. FIND SOMEONE WHO HAS FOUND MONEY AND KEPT IT.

8. FIND SOMEONE WHO HAS BOUGHT SOMETHING, USED IT, AND THEN RETURNED IT.

9. FIND SOMEONE WHO DIDN'T HELP SOMEONE WHO REALLY NEEDED HELP.

10. FIND SOMEONE WHO'S SEEN AN R OR NC-17 MOVIE BEFORE AGE 17.

11. FIND SOMEONE WHO HAS REFUSED TO HELP A YOUNGER SIBLING WITH HOMEWORK.

12. FIND SOMEONE WHO HAS "BORROWED" SOMETHING AND RETURNED IT WITHOUT THE OWNER'S KNOWLEDGE.

13. FIND SOMEONE WHO HAS STAYED OUT LATER THAN HIS OR HER PARENTS SAID WAS OK.

14. FIND SOMEONE WHO DIDN'T SAY ANYTHING WHEN HE OR SHE WAS GIVEN CREDIT FOR SOMETHING SOMEONE ELSE DID.

15. FIND SOMEONE WHO HAS GOTTEN SOMETHING FROM A VENDING MACHINE WITHOUT PUTTING MONEY IN.

16. FIND SOMEONE WHO HASN'T BEEN TOTALLY HONEST WITH SOMEONE SO AS NOT TO HURT THAT PERSON'S FEELINGS.

EXTRA ACTION

Step 2
Instead of giving each group member two slips of paper from Repro Resource 4, give each person a complete sheet. Have everyone, including yourself, look over the sheet and circle the numbers of all the things he or she has done. Then have kids arrange their chairs in a big circle (with no empty chairs anywhere in the circle). You will stand in the middle of the circle. Call out, **Number one.** All those who circled number one on their sheet will get up and sit in another chair. You will also try to sit in a vacant chair. This will leave one person standing. This person should briefly describe the last time he or she did the thing listed on the sheet and explain whether he or she feels it was right or wrong. Then the person will call another number to continue the game.

Step 5
After briefly reviewing some of the situations listed on Repro Resource 4, have group members form teams of three or four. Instruct each team to develop two short skits dealing with an action from Repro Resource 4. In one of the skits, the action should be OK (due to the circumstances in the skit); in the other, it should be wrong. The teams should act out the wrong circumstance first, and the OK one second. Between skits, have the rest of the group members discuss the underlying motives in each circumstance. For example, in one set of skits, Person A might find out that Person B has a drinking problem. Person B may plead with Person A not to tell anyone. In the first skit, Person A might gossip about Person B's problem or make a joke about it. In the second skit, Person A might tell someone out of genuine concern—someone (like a counselor) who might be able help Person B. In both cases, Person A didn't keep the problem a secret, but the motives for telling about it were entirely different.

SMALL GROUP

Step 2
Instead of cutting apart Repro Resource 4 and giving a couple of slips to each person, simply make one copy of it and cut it apart. Have the entire group rank the actions from "most wrong" to "least wrong." As you go through this exercise, find out what criteria kids are using to determine how wrong a certain action is. If kids have difficulty ranking the actions, have them consider which actions would result in the most harm. Don't worry about reaching a consensus; just try to get kids thinking about the difference between right and wrong, and the motives that differentiate the two.

Step 4
With a small group, you might have time to allow for more personal sharing about making difficult choices between right and wrong. Have each group member identify one difficult choice he or she has faced or may face in the future. Use the principles from Galatians 5:16-26 to discuss proper and improper motives for each choice. Here are some examples:
• Going to college or not going to college
• Going to a Christian college or going to a "secular" one
• Going to a party where alcohol is being served or not going
• Buying a new car or a used one
• Whether to continue in a dating relationship or break it off

LARGE GROUP

Step 1
Have group members form teams. Give each team a copy of Repro Resource 3. Team members will work together in completing the sheet (in pencil), crossing off all the misspelled words. When a team thinks it's finished, one member of the team should run up to you. You will look the sheet over and tell the person how many words are still misspelled, if any. But don't say which words are misspelled, and certainly don't tell the person to check the words in the introduction. If words are still misspelled, that team must try again. Continue until one team identifies all the misspelled words.

Step 2
If you have sixteen or more group members, you might want to try this variation for using Repro Resource 4. Give each group member a complete copy of the Repro Resource. (This will save you the hassle of a lot of cutting!) When you say **Go,** kids should circulate and get signatures for as many of the items as they can in five minutes. The catch is that a person may sign only one time on each sheet and may sign only one time for any given number. In other words, once someone has signed next to #1 (driving over the speed limit) on someone's sheet, he or she may not sign next to that item on anyone else's sheet. Also, that person also may not sign next to any of the other numbers on the first person's sheet. If you do it this way, don't expect kids to "discuss" whether the action was right or wrong. You can do that after the signature hunt.

Step 3

The Galatians 5 passage (especially the part about the fruit of the Spirit) may be quite familiar to some of your group members. After having teams brainstorm some modern examples of the actions and attitudes listed in the text, have them list Bible characters (other than Jesus) who exhibited each of these traits. If possible, they should try to think of at least one character for each trait (negative and positive) listed in these verses. Some characters (like David) displayed both negative traits (like sexual immorality) and positive ones (like patience). This activity will not only test how much your kids really know about the Bible, but will also demonstrate how incredibly believable these characters are—and how forgiving God is to those, like David, who asked for His forgiveness.

Step 5

The suggested ending for the session might not cut it among kids who think they've heard it all before. Sure, they'll give the right answers, but will it make any meaningful difference to them? Here's another, more memorable way to make the same point. Have each person write down one act of the sinful nature that he or she is struggling with. No one else in the group, including you, will see what's written. Then have group members fold their pieces of paper and nail them to a piece of wood (preferably shaped as a cross). Spend some time in prayer—both asking for forgiveness, and thanking God for totally removing our sin through Jesus' death on the cross. Then read Psalm 103. Afterward, remove the pieces of paper, tear them up so they can't ever be read, and throw them away. Then distribute new pieces of paper and colorful markers. Have group members write down one of the fruit of the Spirit listed in Galatians 5:22, 23 that they feel most in need of developing in their lives. Encourage them to keep the papers someplace visible during the week.

Step 3

Two basic concepts covered in this session may be confusing to those without much Bible background: sin and the Holy Spirit. While it's impossible to cover both of these concepts in much depth in the limited time you have, you might want to review Romans 8:1-17. This passage provides some excellent tie-ins to the Galatians 5 passage. Make sure everyone understands what Romans 8:9 is saying. If some of your kids question whether or not they have the Spirit of God in them, share with them the plan of salvation. Stress that without God's grace, it would be impossible to live a life totally pleasing to Him. Our sinful nature prevents that. But through Christ's death and resurrection, we can enter into a father-child relationship with God (Romans 8:15, 16). There's no better news than this!

Step 5

Spend some extra time discussing how a person who is living in the Spirit and one who isn't would react differently to the following situations:

- Breakup with a boyfriend or girlfriend.
- Parents' divorce.
- Being diagnosed with a terminal illness.
- Inheriting a bunch of money.

If kids are feeling like there's no way they can be Christians because they keep sinning, review Paul's words in Romans 7:14-25. Point out that this is the same guy who wrote the Galatians 5 passage!

Step 1

If you'd prefer more sharing early in the session, consider having each group member complete the following statements. Group members should write each answer on a separate slip of paper. The statements are as follows:

- **The dumbest thing I've ever done is . . .**
- **The smartest thing I've ever done is . . .**
- **The nicest thing I've ever done is . . .**
- **The most wrong thing I've ever done that I'm willing to talk about is . . .**

Collect the slips of paper, read them one at a time, and have group members guess who said what. Ask kids to elaborate on and explain their responses as necessary. Use the last statement as a lead-in to the subject of right and wrong.

Step 5

Write the following "Psalm starter" on the board. It's taken from Psalm 18:1-3. Have group members fill in the blanks with words of their choosing and then read their finished psalms aloud.

I love you, O Lord, my _______________.
The Lord is my _____________, my
______________ and my _____________;
my God is my ________________, in
whom I _________________________.
I call to the Lord, who is ___________,
and I am ______________________.

MOSTLY GIRLS

Step 3
Have the two teams write their lists on poster board to accommodate discussion with the other team. As the items are listed, ask group members to write next to each one an example of how *they* might demonstrate that action or attitude. For example, next to "idolatry," team members might write "Putting too much emphasis on diet and appearance." Or, next to "goodness," team members might write "Offering to baby-sit for free for someone who really needs it."

Step 4
As you're discussing the "questionable" actions from Repro Resource 3, randomly select one group member to be the "decision maker." After each action is discussed, the decision maker will decide if it is right or wrong. Announce that the decision maker's word is final; no one may disagree with her. Afterward, ask: **How did you feel about this method of determining right and wrong? Do you think it's appropriate for a person to have the final say about such things? What if this person were extremely wise and intelligent—would that make a difference? Explain.**

MOSTLY GUYS

Step 3
Use some of the following questions in discussing the Galatians 5:16-26 passage.
- **If, after reading this passage, someone said, "Christianity sounds awfully boring," how would you respond?**
- **How would you rank the acts of the sinful nature** (vss. 19-21) **according to how common they are among guys you know?**
- **Which of the fruit of the Spirit listed in verses 22 and 23 do you think are most difficult for males in our society to show? Why?**
- **Verse 24 says we are to crucify the sinful nature with its passions and desires. Besides taking cold showers, how can guys do this? Does God really expect us to not have sexual desires? Desires for good health and success? What do you think this verse is saying?**

Step 5
Here's another one of those curriculum suggestions that looks good on paper but might not go over real big with a group of guys. If it works for you, great! If you think your group isn't up to the level of sharing called for in the session, try something else instead. Have each group member write on a slip of paper one sinful desire that he's struggling with. Collect the slips without looking at them. Then, if you can find a safe place (preferably outside), burn them. Have some water on hand, just in case. After burning these slips, give each group member another slip of paper with one of the nine fruit of the Spirit listed on it. Have each guy tell one way he could show that character trait this week. If your group would have trouble with even that much sharing, simply distribute the slips of paper and then spend some time in prayer, asking God to help your group members develop these qualities.

EXTRA FUN

Step 1
OK, we admit that starting the session off with a spelling test isn't exactly what kids consider fun. If you think that smacks too much of school, try another idea. Divide your group into at least two teams (of any size). Give each team a box of Post AlphaBits cereal and a copy of Repro Resource 3. Using the cereal letters, each team will spell out the correct spelling of all the misspelled words on the sheet. Follow the same rules as found in the "Large Group" option for Step 1. This game will work even if there are only two or three members on each team—it just might take a little longer.

Step 5
Since you've been talking about the fruit of the Spirit, play some "fruit games" after the serious part of your session is over. You'll need a large supply of various types of fruit on hand.
- See which team can peel an orange the fastest, using right hands only.
- See which team can most accurately guess what amount of fruit comes closest to five pounds. (If you do this, remember to bring a scale!)
- See which team can make the most creative fruit sculpture, using fruit, toothpicks, and whipped cream.
- If it's summer, have a watermelon seed spitting contest. See who can spit a seed the farthest. If it's not summer, use apple seeds.
- See who can balance a banana on his or her head the longest, while you call out various actions (sit down, jump up and down three times, etc.).

MEDIA

Step 1

Before the session, videotape someone explaining all the correct answers to the spelling quiz on Repro Resource 3. This person could explain about all the misspelled words in the introduction and go through each of the twelve word pairs. To make it more visually interesting, have him or her hold up "A" or "B" answer cards while he or she talks. Add other touches of humor if you're feeling especially creative. One idea would be to have various people from the church walk or run through the background.

During the session, hand out the Repro Resource sheet. Explain to your group members that to make this activity easier, you videotaped all the answers to help them out. Then play the tape—at fast-forward speed. Have group members take the test while you rewind the tape. Make the point later in the session that sometimes it's hard to tell right from wrong because things are moving too fast. When kids are finished taking the test, replay the tape at the proper speed and let them grade their papers.

Step 3

Instead of having kids merely list modern examples of each action or attitude, have them comb through old newspapers and newsmagazines for examples of each one. In all likelihood, those looking for negative actions/attitudes will have an easier time. If this is the case, use this as an opportunity to ask group members what this says about our society. To add a little more interest to this activity, have one team locate the stories and have the other team guess which attitude/action from Galatians 5 it represents.

SHORT MEETING TIME

Step 1

Instead of giving everyone a copy of Repro Resource 3, stage a quick spelling bee. Have group members form two teams. Instruct each team to write down the correct spelling of the words that you select (either from the sheet or words of your own choosing). See which team gets the most correct answers. To add even more interest, give each team ten points to start with. Let them "wager" as many points as they want based on how sure they are of the correctness of their word. If they are right, add that many points to their score; if they are wrong, deduct that many points. See which team ends up with the most points. Award a team prize, if you want. Be careful not to play too many rounds—you can always play more rounds after you get through the important parts of the session!

Step 2

The activity involving Repro Resource 4 may take more time than you have. If this is the case, simply read through the items listed on the sheet and have kids "vote" on whether each item is right or wrong. The easiest way to vote would be through a show of hands. A more fun option would be to have kids show the strength of their opinions by how high they raise their hands. If they think the action is really wrong, their hands should be raised as high as possible. If they think the action is really right, they should hold their hands as low to the floor as possible. Don't settle for any "it depends" answers at this point.

URBAN

Step 1

Point out that in answering the question "How do we determine whether an action is good or bad, right or wrong?" another question we must consider is "What would Jesus have me do in this situation?" Give group members a chance to apply these questions to the following scenarios.

(1) Shekiesha is a brilliant, church-going sixteen-year-old senior heading to Spelman College in the fall to study law. After her senior prom, she and her boyfriend Ramon had sex for the first time. Now it's July, and Shekiesha has just discovered she's two months pregnant. She's supposed to leave for college in a month. Since no one knows of her condition but her, Shekiesha is considering having an abortion. If Shekiesha asked herself, "What would Jesus have me do in this situation?" what response might she come up with?

(2) Johnny Hawkeye is a fifteen-year-old Hopi Indian from Phoenix, Arizona. Two nights ago he witnessed a gang murder from his third-story window. When the police asked for witnesses, as always, those who saw something told the police they didn't for fear of retaliation. If Johnny asked himself, "What would Jesus have me do in this situation?" how might he respond?

Step 2

To make Repro Resource 4 more applicable to an urban group, you might change #1 from "Find someone who has driven at least ten miles per hour over the speed limit" to "Find someone who has bought something on the street without asking where it came from." You might also add the following suggestion: "Find someone who has watched a drug deal go down without reporting it."

JR.HIGH HIGH SCHOOL COMBINED

Step 4

Younger adolescents may have difficulty relating to many of the actions listed on Repro Resource 4. Instead of going through these, bring in some of the following things: teen-oriented magazines, a recent top 40 radio listing, a page from the newspaper listing current movies, and a television listing guide. Have group members form teams of two or three. Instruct each team to go through the items, searching for (1) examples of things (ads, song titles, program descriptions) that seem to be satisfying our sinful human nature, (2) things that seem to be satisfying the Spirit, and (3) things that there might be disagreements about. After a few minutes, have the teams share their lists. See if everyone else agrees with the categories in which things were placed.

Step 5

Junior highers may feel threatened by breaking into pairs and sharing attitudes they need to develop/eliminate. If you feel that's the case with your group, have each group member write down one attitude he or she needs to develop, and one he or she needs to work on eliminating. If none of the attitudes you listed earlier seem to fit, encourage kids to come up with other ones. Collect all the responses, making sure to keep the two types of responses separate. Then divide into two teams: the Good Attitudes and the Bad Attitudes. Play a few rounds of "hangman," in which you select one word or phrase from each type of response and see which team uses the fewest guesses to solve its word. The Good Attitudes will guess words you've selected from the attitudes we need to develop, and the Bad Attitudes will guess words from the attitudes we need to eliminate.

EXTRA CHALLENGE

Step 3

Here are some questions to help you go deeper into the Galatians 5:16-26 passage.

- **In verse 18, what is the phrase "you are not under law" referring to? What law is it talking about?**
- **Is verse 21 saying that alcoholics, people who struggle with sexual immorality, and people who struggle with some of these other issues won't make it to heaven? If not, what is it saying?** (You might also have group members look up I Corinthians 6:9-11 and Ephesians 5:5 for further insight.)
- **Why do you think the qualities in verses 22 and 23 are listed in the order they are in? How does this listing of virtues compare to those found in II Corinthians 6:6; Ephesians 4:2; 5:9; and Colossians 3:12-15?**
- **What do you suppose the last part of verse 23 is saying?**
- **If the sinful nature has been crucified** (vs. 24)**, do you think that means Christians no longer struggle with the types of things listed in verses 19-21? Why or why not?**
- **How can we "keep in step with the Spirit"** (vs. 25)**?**

Step 5

Making the two lists on the board might seem redundant, especially if you talked about the attitudes in your earlier study of the Galatians passage. A more challenging wrap-up would be to have each group member develop an action plan for keeping in step with the Spirit. This plan should include the following:

- statement of purpose (what it means to live in the Spirit)
- objectives (at least two or three major goals)
- strategies (specific ways of meeting each objective)

Have group members share their plans with each other and hold each other accountable to them.

PLANNING CHECKLIST

Date Used:

Approx. Time

Step 1: Spelling Bee Real ______
o Large Group
o Fellowship & Worship
o Extra Fun
o Media
o Short Meeting Time
o Urban
Things needed:

Step 2: Who's Been Bad or Good? ______
o Extra Action
o Small Group
o Large Group
o Short Meeting Time
o Urban
Things needed:

Step 3: Who Are We Trying to Please? ______
o Heard It All Before
o Little Bible Background
o Mostly Girls
o Mostly Guys
o Media
o Extra Challenge
Things needed:

Step 4: Another Look ______
o Small Group
o Mostly Girls
o Combined Junior High/High School
Things needed:

Step 5: By His Spirit ______
o Extra Action
o Heard It All Before
o Little Bible Background
o Fellowship & Worship
o Mostly Guys
o Extra Fun
o Combined Junior High/High School
o Extra Challenge
Things needed:

SESSION

3

If Sin Is Fun, Why Stay Clean?

YOUR GOALS FOR THIS SESSION:

Choose one or more

- [ ] To help kids recognize how easily we can be tempted by certain things.
- [ ] To help kids understand why it's important to resist temptation to do wrong things.
- [ ] To help kids focus on Psalm 121 when facing temptation.
- [ ] Other ______________________________

Your Bible Base:

Psalm 121
II Corinthians 5:1-10; 6:14–7:2

STEP 1

For the Love of Money

(Needed: A twenty-dollar bill)

OPTIONS

EXTRA ACTION

EXTRA FUN

MEDIA

Hold up a twenty-dollar bill. Ask the following questions, waiting for group members' responses after each one.

How many of you would jump out of a second-story window for this twenty-dollar bill?

How many of you would kiss a dog on the nose for this twenty-dollar bill?

How many of you would eat worms for this twenty-dollar bill?

How many of you would lie to your mother for this twenty-dollar bill?

Ask volunteers to call out the most extreme things they would do for the twenty-dollar bill.

After several group members have responded, ask: **What makes this twenty-dollar bill so attractive?** (Responses might include the following: "It would buy a lot of gas for my car"; "I could buy a new CD with it"; "I just like money"; etc.)

Why would some of us be willing to do dumb, embarrassing, repulsive, or even dishonest things to get a twenty-dollar bill? (Some group members may say that any embarrassment is worth $20. Others may say they need the money because they're desperate. Still others may say they like challenges, and they view doing something embarrassing for money as a challenge.)

Explain: **Some things are so attractive and desirable to us that we will do or give up almost anything to get them. And sometimes that can lead to trouble.**

use Matthew Williams' Comparison of Sin to Ice.

STEP 2

What Temptations?

(Needed: Copies of Repro Resource 5, pencils)

Distribute a copy of "The Temptations" (Repro Resource 5) and a pencil to each group member. Explain: **Today we're going to be talking about things that tempt us to do wrong. And we're going to start out by getting personal. On your sheet, I want you to rate each of these temptations in terms of how tempting that thing is to you. Whatever it is, be honest.**

Don't write your names on your papers, and don't include any information that might identify who you are.

Give group members a few minutes to work. When they're finished, collect the sheets, shuffle them, and then summarize some of the major temptations aloud.

See if there is any consensus among your group members concerning the things that are generally tempting to them. These things might include entertaining sexual fantasies, looking at pornography, drinking alcoholic beverages, taking drugs, making fun of others, etc. If this is the case with your group, mention it. Then ask volunteers to explain why these things are so tempting to so many people. Encourage several group members to respond.

Then ask: **What is it that makes some temptations so hard to resist?** (Many temptations promise immediate fun. Turning them down can make a person feel "boring" or "old-fashioned." Often, the pressure of friends encourages people to give in to temptation.)

Why do you think God allows us to face temptations in our lives? Let group members speculate for a few minutes.

To complicate the issue, you might ask questions such as the following: **Does He allow us to face temptation to build our character? Does He do it to keep us from enjoying our time on earth too much? Is He not able to prevent us from facing temptation?** Get a few more responses.

Then ask: **Why should we resist these temptations? What's the big deal about giving in to them every once in a while?** Encourage honest, specific answers. For instance, if someone says, "We shouldn't give in to temptation because God tells us not to," ask the person to show you specific Scripture references to back up his or her opinion.

After several group members have offered their opinions, say: **Let's**

O P T I O N S

go straight to the source for our answers. Let's take a look at what the Bible says.

STEP
3

Why Try?

(Needed: Bibles, chalkboard and chalk or newsprint and marker)

Instruct group members to read II Corinthians 5:1-10; 6:14–7:2. Write the passage on the board so group members can refer to it. When everyone is finished reading, ask: **What reasons are given in these verses for resisting temptation?** (Answers may not be immediately obvious, especially since some of these verses aren't that familiar. You may need to direct kids' attention to 5:10 and 7:1. II Corinthians 5:10 suggests that we will someday be judged for our actions. Fearing this judgment might cause us to think twice before giving in to temptation. II Corinthians 7:1 offers another motivation—reverence, or gratitude to God. This positive motivation can also be seen in 5:9 where it's stated that our goal is to please God.)

Say: **Christians might give many different reasons for why it's important to resist temptations. But most of these reasons can be boiled down to two: either to avoid God's punishment or to demonstrate our thankfulness to God for all that He's done for us.**

Where do you stand on this issue? When you resist temptations to do wrong, what's your primary motivation—to escape punishment or to show your appreciation to God? Encourage several group members to respond honestly.

Read aloud II Corinthians 5:1-10; 6:14–7:2 and have group members consider the words of the passage again. See if anyone has any questions about the verses.

Then ask: **What difference does it make what our motivation is, as long as we resist temptation?** If no one mentions it, point out that it's a matter of attitude. People who resist because they're afraid of punishment may do so grudgingly. People who resist out of thankfulness will do so joyfully.

Why should we want to please God? (He's done so much for us. He created us. He gave us free wills to make our own choices. When our choices led to sin and destroyed our relationship with Him, He sent His Son to die in our place so that our relationship with Him

OPTIONS

When we give in to temptation, or comprimise our witness is damaged. What we believe in is even more unbelieveable to an unbeliever than it might have been before.

could be restored. He protects us and watches out for us all the time. In comparison, simply doing what He asks us to do seems like a minor sacrifice.)

Suggest that viewing temptations as opportunities to show our appreciation to God may take away some of the allure of those temptations, and might make them easier to resist. There's certainly more to holiness than saying no to certain temptations, but our ability to deal with temptation is one outward sign of inward holiness.

Say: **The Scripture passages we looked at indicate that the rewards for resisting temptation far exceed the benefits we might receive for giving in to temptation. Let's take a look at how this really works.**

STEP 4

Give In or Resist?

(Needed: Copies of Repro Resource 6, pencils)

Distribute copies of "Temptation Ayes" (Repro Resource 6) and pencils. Give group members about ten minutes to work through the sheet individually.

For the last two exercises on the sheet, group members are asked to fill in temptations from their own lives that they've faced or that they are facing. To help spark group members' brainstorming, you may want to briefly review some of the temptations they discussed in Step 2.

After group members have completed the sheet, go through the situations one at a time. Have several volunteers share the benefits they came up with for giving in to the temptation and for resisting the temptation.

Use the following information to supplement group members' responses.

Drinking

Benefits of giving in—Fitting in with other people who drink; feeling the "buzz" of being drunk; being able to forget about your worries and problems for a while; being thought of as "cool," "wild," or "fearless"

Benefits of resisting—Maintaining control of your senses; being able to prove to others that you don't need alcohol to have fun; keeping yourself safe from other temptations that come with blurred thinking; avoiding hangovers; pleasing God

OPTIONS

Cheating

Benefits of giving in—Improving your grades; being able to spend your time doing things other than studying; being able to help friends get good grades too

Benefits of resisting—Not having to worry about being caught; being able to say you earned the grade you got; learning important information through studying; pleasing God

Having premarital sex

Benefits of giving in—Physical pleasure and satisfaction; being able to satisfy your curiosity; the feeling of being close to someone or of being loved, even if the feeling is temporary

Benefits of resisting—Not having to worry about pregnancy; not having to worry about AIDS or any other sexually transmitted diseases; being able to give the gift of your virginity to your spouse on your wedding night; pleasing God

Abusing drugs

Benefits of giving in—Feeling the high that drugs give; fitting in with others who do drugs; being able to forget about your worries and problems for a while; being thought of as "cool," "wild," or "fearless"; satisfying your curiosity about what drugs are like

Benefits of resisting—Not having to worry about overdosing; not having to worry about getting addicted; not having to worry about getting caught; pleasing God

Putting someone down

Benefits of giving in—Having other people think you're funny or cool; fitting in with others who put people down

Benefits of resisting—Not having people get mad at you for something you said; pleasing God

For the last two situations on the sheet, ask for volunteers to read what they wrote. If no one wants to share about his or her personal temptations, that's OK. Don't pressure anyone to respond.

Afterward, say: **Some of these things that tempt us can seem very alluring. Sometimes they may even seem too good to pass up. But we need to weigh the consequences very thoroughly and make the decision to resist. We can be sure that God will help us make the right decisions—and help us carry them out.**

STEP 5

No Slipping Feet

(Needed: Bible, business cards or slips of paper the size of business cards, pencils)

Read aloud Psalm 121 while group members follow along in their Bibles. Then ask: **How do the words of this psalm relate to resisting temptation?** (God can keep us from slipping. He's always ready to help. He protects us.)

Distribute slips of paper and pencils. (If you have business cards with your name and number or the church's phone number on them, distribute those.) Have group members look again at Psalm 121 and choose one verse from it that seems particularly helpful to them. Have them copy that verse onto the slip of paper or back of the business card.

Then say: **Whenever you think of it, take a look at this verse. Let it sink into your mind so that you will remember it whenever you're tempted to do something you know you shouldn't.**

To help group members begin using these verses, have them pair up. Instruct them to read their verses to their partners and explain why they chose the verses they did.

When everyone is finished, close the session in prayer, asking God to help your group members as He promises to do in Psalm 121.

Memorize the verse they Chose.

OPTIONS

SMALL GROUP

LITTLE BIBLE BACKGROUND

FELLOWSHIP & WORSHIP

MOSTLY GUYS

EXTRA FUN

JR. HIGH HIGH SCHOOL COMBINED

EXTRA CHALLENGE

THE TEMPTATIONS

Here's a list of several things that tempt people. For each one, rate how tempting that item is for you. Then put a star by one or two items on the list that are most tempting to you.

	No Sweat	Minor Temptation	Major Temptation
Cheating at school			
Stealing/shoplifting			
Drinking alcoholic beverages			
Taking drugs			
Smoking			
Gossiping			
Lying			
Losing my temper			
Making fun of others			
Entertaining sexual fantasies			
Looking at pornography			
Having sex outside of marriage			
Buying more than I need			
Being jealous of someone else			
Eating more than I should			
Being lazy			

TEMPTATION AYES

For each of the temptations below, list the possible benefits of giving in to the temptation and the possible benefits of resisting the temptation. The first example has some answers listed to get you started. Add to it other things you think of.

The last two temptations are left blank. In those spaces, list temptations that are real to you right now. Then fill in the benefits concerning those temptations.

TEMPTATION	BENEFITS OF GIVING IN	BENEFITS OF RESISTING
Drinking	• Fitting in with other people who drink • Feeling the "buzz" of being drunk • Being able to forget about your worries and problems for a while	• Maintaining control of your senses • Keeping yourself safe from other temptations that come with blurred thinking • Avoiding hangovers • Pleasing God
Cheating		
Having premarital sex		
Abusing drugs		
Putting someone down		

EXTRA ACTION

Step 1
Instead of using a twenty-dollar bill, offer something you're really willing to part with (perhaps a one-dollar bill or a bag of M&Ms). See who's willing to do the dumbest, most embarrassing, repulsive, or exhausting thing to win the prize. Have kids suggest things they'd be willing to do to win the prize. Have them try to better each other; then decide which one gets the prize—after he or she performs what he or she promised to do. Here are some suggestions group members might consider: doing fifty push-ups, singing a solo, drinking lemon juice, balancing a beanbag on one's head for the rest of the session, etc. Afterward, ask: **What, if anything, does this exercise tell us about temptation?** (We sometimes do stupid things to get what we want. We continue to "up the ante" in order to get more pleasure out of the temptation.) Adapt other questions as you see fit.

Step 3
When you ask, **Where do you stand on this issue?** instead of having group members answer verbally, set up a continuum in your room for them to answer physically. Designate one side of the room to represent the argument that we should resist temptation to avoid God's punishment. Designate the other side of the room to represent the argument that we should resist temptation out of thankfulness to God. Instruct group members to choose a spot in the room that indicates their beliefs. They may choose to stand on either side of the room, or they may choose to stand somewhere between the two extremes. However, discourage anyone from standing exactly in the middle of the continuum. Everyone should show some preference one way or the other. After everyone has chosen a spot, ask volunteers to explain why they're standing where they are.

SMALL GROUP

Step 2
In a small group, kids may fear that you'll be able to figure out which temptations they checked on Repro Resource 5. Instead have group members come up with a ranking of the top five or ten temptations that people their age face. Have each group member list on a sheet of paper what he or she considers to be the top five temptations other kids face. Collect the sheets and quickly tally the responses. See if there are any temptations that appear on most lists. Spend some time focusing on those specific items. Ask: **Are there any temptations that should have been added to this list?**

Step 5
If your group is close-knit, have each person share one temptation he or she struggles with a lot right now. Encourage honest and open sharing, but don't force anyone to say something if he or she isn't ready to. Encourage those who are uncomfortable to speak very generally about the temptations they face. You should share first. This is a great chance for you to model openness by sharing some of your own struggles. Your own example will set the tone for what others share. Kids need to see that adults continue to struggle with temptations. When closing in prayer, spend some concentrated time on each individual in the group. You should simply call out each person's name and then have kids pray silently or aloud for that person before you call out the next name.

LARGE GROUP

Step 2
After having kids go through Repro Resource 5 individually, divide into teams. Instruct the members of each team to come up with a list of the top three temptations people their age face. Then have each team compose one or more nursery rhymes to describe the temptations. (For example: "Jack and Jill went up the hill to park their car in the moonlight. When Jack said, "More," Jill ran out the door—and didn't date Jack thereafter.") If group members don't want to use nursery rhymes, have them write limericks. (For example: "There once was a girl from Wheeling, who wanted to look quite appealing. She went to the mall, and had a great fall—when Security noticed her stealing.") When the teams are finished, have each one share its list and nursery rhyme/limerick with the rest of the group.

Step 4
To add more individual interest to the activity, have group members form teams of three or four. Instruct half of the teams to list the benefits of giving in to one or more of the temptations on Repro Resource 6. Instruct the other teams to list the benefits of resisting one or more of the temptations. After a few minutes, stage a series of debates, tackling one issue at a time. Explain that in a debate, you don't necessarily have to believe in a position to argue for it. You will moderate the debate, playing devil's advocate when necessary. Here are some things you could say from time to time to keep the discussion lively:

- **Just because it's wrong for you doesn't mean it's wrong for everyone.**
- **That's what my grandparents would say. Get real.**
- **It's not really wrong if nobody gets hurt, is it?**

If you use statements like these, make sure that kids understand that you're merely using them to spark discussion.

Step 3

Arrange in advance to have some adults visit your group, or to have your group go someplace else in the church where adults are meeting (or standing around). Have each group member ask at least one adult this question: "Why should we resist temptation?" Instruct group members to write down the answers verbatim. After collecting several responses, try to categorize them into the two basic motivations: to avoid punishment or to show appreciation to God. If you don't have time to do this, or if there aren't enough adults available, have your group members categorize the following responses:

- "Because God tells us to."
- "It's God's will."
- "To stay out of trouble."
- "The Bible tells us to."
- "So we don't sin."
- "Because Jesus did."
- "To prevent a downward spiral."
- "It makes God happy."

Step 4

Invite some adults who have struggled with various temptations to talk about the benefits of giving in versus resisting—from their perspective. Make sure the people you invite are comfortable talking about their experiences. You'll probably have difficulty finding someone who's willing to talk about pornography, or other more "secret" temptations. But maybe you know people who are in recovery from drug abuse or alcoholism. Maybe you know someone who became pregnant before marriage. If these people are willing to talk about their experiences, and you think they might be able to help your kids, then the personal experiences they share will speak much louder to your kids than simply filling out another work sheet. Another possibility would be to have a Christian counselor come and share about the relationship between temptation and sin, especially pertaining to addictions.

Step 3

Before launching into the II Corinthians passage, you might want to provide a little background about temptation. Consider emphasizing three points.

1. Temptation can be positive or negative. In James 1:2-4, we are to consider it pure joy when we face trials and testing. The Greek word for "trials" is the same as that translated "tempted" in verse 13. In this sense, temptations help to strengthen us and make us mature. James 1:13-15 show the negative side of temptation. Note the downward slide—evil desire leads to sin which leads to death.
2. Temptation isn't the same as sin. Jesus was tempted in every way that we are but was without sin (Hebrews 4:15). Temptation becomes sin when we accept the suggestion of evil and entertain thoughts of doing something evil, or actually give in to the temptation.
3. It's possible to resist temptation. God provides a way out if we're willing to accept it (I Corinthians 10:13).

Step 5

Have kids look for key words in Psalm 121. In the NIV, the word "Lord" and the phrase "watch(es) over" each occur five times. Spend some time discussing how it feels to know that God is watching over everything we do. Do your group members think it's a positive thing or a negative thing? Ask: **Why does the Lord watch over us in this way?** Help kids see that He watches over us for our own benefit, not to "zap" us when He catches us doing wrong. Tie this concept back to our basic motivation for resisting temptation. If we view God as a cosmic Santa Claus ("He sees you when you're sleeping; He knows when you're awake. . . ."), then our motivation will be to escape punishment. But if we view Him as a loving parent trying to protect us from harm, then our motivation to resist temptation will be more out of gratitude to Him.

Step 4

Put copies of Repro Resource 4 at various locations around your room. Highlight on each sheet which of the temptations should be discussed at that location. Assign kids to as many teams as you have locations. Assign each team a location. Have each team list one benefit of resisting and one benefit of giving in to the temptation highlighted on the sheet at that location. When each team is done, have half of the group members rotate right and half rotate left. These new teams should then add another benefit under each category. Keep going until everyone's been to all locations.

Step 5

Have your group members form two teams. The teams will read Psalm 121 aloud. One team will read all the even-numbered verses; the other will read all of the odd-numbered verses. To make this activity even more memorable, have each team rewrite its verses, thinking especially about how they relate to temptation. Then come back together for the responsive reading.

Here's one possible rendering of the first two verses to get you started:

"When I'm feeling down, I look at something beautiful the Lord has made and ask myself if He'll be able to help me once again.

"The Lord always comes through for me. If He can make the heaven and earth, He can certainly help me."

MOSTLY GIRLS

Step 2

To provide a little more anonymity and perhaps to encourage group members to be more open in their responses, try a variation of the Repro Resource activity. Distribute two slips of paper and a pencil to each group member. Instruct group members to write down the most pressing temptation they face on one slip and the most pressing temptation one of their friends faces on the other slip. Collect the slips and tally the results on the board.

Step 3

As you're discussing reasons for resisting temptation, add a third choice to the mix: "Because someone else said I should." Say: **Some of you may not always think about God when you're faced with temptation. Perhaps you resist temptation to stay out of trouble with your parents, teachers, or some other authority figure. How many of you would say you fit in this category?** If you think group members would be hesitant to admit this by raising their hand, have them fill out slips of paper instead. Afterward, discuss whether this third option is a proper motivation for resisting temptation.

MOSTLY GUYS

Step 4

If your group is made up entirely of guys, this might be a great opportunity to deal honestly with some of the sexual temptations they are facing. Hand out some blank sheets of paper. Instruct the guys to write down some of their questions about sexual temptation. If this is too risky, you might want to prepare some questions beforehand. For instance: **How would you respond to each of the following statements?**

- **A lot of girls are trying to tempt us sexually.**
- **It's better to masturbate than burn with lust.**
- **Pornography keeps people from getting sexually transmitted diseases.**
- **It just isn't cool to be a virgin.**
- **Sex is OK so long as it's safe.**

Step 5

Some guys may find this closing step a bit hokey. Simply read Psalm 121 and ask how it would help a guy facing the following temptations:

- To lie to a parent.
- To cheat on a test.
- To get paid for more work than he actually does.
- To go further sexually than he knows is right.
- To put someone down behind his or her back.
- To get drunk with his friends.
- To take steroids so he can look stronger.

Then discuss ways we can "lift our eyes to the Lord." Ask: **How can we do this in our daily lives?**

EXTRA FUN

Step 1

Send out invitations to this session or post flyers with the session title, "If Sin Is Fun, Why Stay Clean?" on them. Feel free to photocopy the art of the pigs frolicking in the mud on the first page of this session. To make the invitations even more memorable, make sure they're nice and dirty before sending or posting them. Step on them with dirty shoes, spill some coffee on them—the messier the better. To keep with this theme, make sure your meeting room is dirty before you meet. Spill some trash, sprinkle a little dirt here and there, "rearrange" the furniture, etc. Have some cleaning supplies on hand. See if any kids take action to clean up the room before you get started.

Step 5

After your session, stage some of the following "clean it up" relays:

- Have group members form teams. Place two trash cans with some paper wads lying around them at one end of the room. Each team member will run to the trash can and put one paper wad in it using only his or her feet. Then he or she will run back and tag the next player, who will do the same.
- Give each team a trash bag and five minutes to go outside and collect as much trash (from the ground, not other trash cans) as possible.
- Give each team a bottle of window cleaner and some paper towels. See which team can clean the most windows in five minutes. Make sure you inspect the teams' work.
- Give each team a broom and an irregular-shaped object (a potato, a small football, a walnut, etc.). The first member from each team will sweep the object to the far side of the room, go around a chair, and return, handing the broom to the next person in line.

Step 1

Before the session, record a number of television commercials. Show them at the start of your meeting. Have kids rate them according to how tempting they are in terms of making people want to use the products being advertised. Some excellent candidates would include ads for perfume and/or cologne, beer, soft drinks, gym shoes, fast food, and ads for television shows. Use questions like the following to direct the discussion to the subject of temptation:

- **How tempting is this ad?**
- **Do you think this ad will make people want this product? If so, why? If not, then why do you think it's being shown? Who would it appeal to?**
- **What types of ads get your attention the most? Why?**

Step 4

Before the session, use a camcorder to videotape several people's responses to the following question: "What words of wisdom do you have for members of my youth group for the next time they are facing the temptation to ____________?" Here are some possible interview subjects and topics:

- Drinking—bartenders, police officers
- Cheating—school teachers, CPAs
- Premarital sex—parents, pastors or other church leaders
- Abusing drugs—doctors, pharmacists
- Putting someone down—a young person from another school or race, or with a disability.

Make sure the interviews are short and well paced. You might want to focus on just one or two areas. During this part of the session, show the interviews and have kids comment on them. This would probably be most effective *after* kids have spent a few minutes thinking about the Repro Resource, but in some cases, it might work well before you hand out the sheets. You make the call.

Step 2

Instead of handing out a copy of Repro Resource 5 to each group member, simply read through the items on the sheet and have kids vote as to whether they think it's a major temptation, minor temptation, or no sweat to most kids their age. You may lose some honesty and openness by doing it this way, and your focus will be less personal. It's always safer to talk about "most kids your age" than about you yourself—especially when talking about temptation!

Step 4

Talk through Repro Resource 6 immediately after handing it out. You can save a few minutes by going through both columns of the sheet as a group, rather than giving some time to work on the sheet individually. Look at both sides of each temptation before moving on to the next one. Even if you're trying to save on time, don't gloss over the benefits of giving in. Since you're at church, kids will expect to hear all about the benefits of resisting temptation. If your discussion of the other side of the equation is honest, they'll know that there's room in your group to deal honestly with these issues.

Another way to save time would be to simply stick with the items that are suggested on the sheet, and not write in two others. Encourage kids to take these sheets home and go through the same exercise for two other temptations they face. If you reward them somehow at the start of your next session for having done this, you'll be more likely to get them to do it.

Step 2

Try a "chilling" activity to help city teens "crack temptation." Bring a hammer and a bag of ice cubes. Ask for two volunteers to compete in an ice-cracking contest. One volunteer will use his or her mouth to crack the ice cubes; the other will use the hammer. Give each contestant five ice cubes. The first one to completely break apart (merely "chipping" the cubes doesn't count) all five of his or her cubes is the winner. To make things a little more even, you may want to give the person using his or her mouth a 30-second head start. Even with the head start, the person using his or her mouth will probably be no match for the person with the hammer. Afterward, say: **There are two ways we can deal with temptation. We can either try to face it alone or we can call on God's strength, which is like a hammer. Using our ice-cracking contest as an object lesson, which would you say is the best way to handle temptation? Why?** Have someone read aloud Jeremiah 23:29.

Step 4

On "Temptation Ayes" (Repro Resource 6), include the category of "Throwing trash on the ground." This daily urban temptation has dramatic environmental repercussions.

Benefits of Giving In

- Trash is gone immediately.
- Someone else takes care of it.
- Breaking glass and littering can be fun.

Benefits of Resisting

- Cleaner community
- Less bacterial disease
- Cleaner air (no stench)
- Make money recycling

JR. HIGH / HIGH SCHOOL COMBINED

Step 2
After going through Repro Resource 5, have kids discuss whether they think temptation is worse in junior high, high school, or college, and why. Ask: **How do temptations differ among these age-groups? How are they similar? If you were to rank the top three temptations on the sheet for each age-group, would the list be the same or different? What other temptations would you add to the list for each age-group?**

Step 5
If younger group members seem to be having difficulty coming up with a single verse that is meaningful to them, make a list on the board of all the qualities or characteristics about God that this verse teaches. Have kids select one of these qualities to write down. Junior highers may be hesitant to pair up with another person and share what they've written on their cards. To get around this, stay together as a group and only have individuals share who are comfortable doing so. When praying, don't expect most junior highers to pray out loud. To encourage them to begin this practice, you might want to offer up some simple sentence starters, and have kids call out one-word responses. Examples: "Lord, it really helps to know you are so . . ." "Help us deal with temptations like . . ." Another way to get them praying out loud would be to "pray" Psalm 121 back to God. Examples: "Thanks, Lord, that we can lift our eyes to the quiet hills and that You give us help . . ." "Thanks that You keep us from all harm . . ."

EXTRA CHALLENGE

Step 3
If your group wants to get deeper into the II Corinthians text, ask:
- **How do you feel about the fact that Paul compares our bodies to tents** (5:1)**? Do you think most people view their bodies this way? How about you?**
- **Do you think most people your age really long for their heavenly dwelling** (5:2, 8)**? Why or why not?**
- **What does it mean to be "clothed" and "unclothed"** (5:3, 4)**?**
- **What is II Corinthians 5:6 saying? Does it mean that the Lord isn't with us here on earth?**
- **If you thought about these verses next time you're tempted, what difference, if any, would it make?**
- **What does II Corinthians 6:14–7:2 say about who you should hang around with? What about who you should date? Does this mean we shouldn't even associate with non-Christians?**
- **If Jesus were writing a commentary on these verses, what do you think He might say? Didn't He sometimes hang out with "unclean" or "unbelieving" people?**

Step 5
Psalm 121 is an ideal psalm to memorize! Assign each person (or team) one of the eight verses. Give each person (team) a piece of paper, scissors, tape, and a stack of magazines. Have group members cut out pictures that remind them of the content of their verse. For example, the pictures for the first verse might include an eye, a hill or mountain, and a question mark. Afterward, put the verses in order, and practice reciting them with the visual clues. After memorizing the verses, ask: **What if you recited this psalm the next time you faced a difficult temptation? Do you think it would help? Explain. What if you recited this psalm right after giving in to temptation? Would it help then? Explain.**

PLANNING CHECKLIST

Date Used:

Approx. Time

Step 1: For the Love of Money ______
o Extra Action
o Extra Fun
o Media
Things needed:

Step 2: What Temptations? ______
o Small Group
o Large Group
o Mostly Girls
o Short Meeting Time
o Urban
o Combined Junior High/High School
Things needed:

Step 3: Why Try? ______
o Extra Action
o Heard It All Before
o Little Bible Background
o Mostly Girls
o Extra Challenge
Things needed:

Step 4: Give In or Resist? ______
o Large Group
o Heard It All Before
o Fellowship & Worship
o Mostly Guys
o Media
o Short Meeting Time
o Urban
Things needed:

Step 5: No Slipping Feet ______
o Small Group
o Little Bible Background
o Fellowship & Worship
o Mostly Guys
o Extra Fun
o Combined Junior High/High School
o Extra Challenge
Things needed:

SESSION 4

Resisting the Wrong

YOUR GOALS FOR THIS SESSION:

Choose one or more

- [ ] To help kids recognize that resisting temptation isn't always easy.
- [ ] To help kids understand how to prepare for and resist the temptations they will face.
- [ ] To help kids commit to seeking God's help when they face temptations.
- [ ] Other ______________________________
____

Your Bible Base:

Matthew 4:1-11
I Corinthians 9:24—10:13

STEP 1

Tempting Setup

(Needed: Copies of Repro Resource 7, pencils, one copy of Repro Resource 8, bite-size candy bars)

OPTIONS

LARGE GROUP
FELLOWSHIP & WORSHIP
EXTRA FUN
MEDIA
SHORT MEETING TIME

You'll need to set up this activity in advance with one of your group members. Tell this person what you're planning, and work together to pull it off.

Before the session, make copies of "Holiness Quiz" (Repro Resource 7) for all of your group members. Also make one copy of "Holiness Quiz Answer Key" (Repro Resource 8).

To begin the session, explain to your group members that you're going to have a quiz to see how much they remember from the previous three sessions of this study.

[NOTE: If you haven't used all three of the previous sessions, or if several of your group members were absent when those sessions were presented, announce that you're going to have a quiz to see how much your group members know about temptation.]

Announce that the prizes for answering questions correctly are candy bars. Each person will receive one small candy bar for each question he or she answers correctly.

As you start to hand out the quizzes, you will "suddenly remember" that you left the candy bars in your car (or in another part of the building). Tell your group to work silently on the quiz while you go to get the candy. Leave the room immediately. When you do, make sure you leave your copy of the answer sheet somewhere in the room, preferably in plain sight.

After you leave, the group member with whom you planned earlier should "find" the answer sheet and try to get others to go over it with him or her. The group member should be sure to warn others not to tell about finding the answer sheet.

When you return to the room, make enough noise to let group members know you're on your way, so that you don't catch them looking at the answer key.

As group members work on the quiz, refuse to answer any questions or respond to any comments. If some people start to tell you what happened, tell them to hold their comments until later.

When group members are finished, go over the answers to the quiz. Then distribute prizes accordingly.

Afterward, ask: **Did anybody cheat on this quiz?** Wait for confessions or accusations. But don't press or accuse group members who don't confess.

Say: **This quiz was a phony. The temptation to cheat was a setup.** Explain how you and your assistant planned the activity before the session began.

Then say: **Temptation itself is what we really want to talk about today. How many of you were tempted to study the answer key?** Encourage group members to respond honestly.

How many of you realized you were being tempted to do something wrong?

How do we recognize temptations and stop ourselves before we do something wrong? Encourage several group members to respond.

Then say: **Don't feel too bad if you gave in to the temptation today. But remember this experience. And dig into this session as we try to learn more about how to recognize and resist temptations.**

[NOTE: The previous session dealt with *why* we should resist temptation. This session focuses on *how* to resist it. Again, there's more to holiness than resisting temptation, but it's certainly a big part of it.]

STEP 2

Tantalizing Temptations

(Needed: Repro Resource 9, pencils)

Distribute a copy of "How Tempting!" (Repro Resource 9) to each group member. Have group members look over each case study and write down the person's options at the two different stages of the story.

After a few minutes, discuss each situation. Focus on the person's temptations, options, and probable consequences.

Ask: **What were some of Carla's options before she agreed to go to the club?** (She could say no; she could explain about her new faith in Christ; she could say yes.)

Why do you think she agreed to go? (Maybe she didn't want to seem like a jerk to her friends. Maybe she really did think she could be a witness to her friends, though it's doubtful whether the club would be a good place for serious conversation.)

What temptations is Carla facing at the club? (She's tempted to compromise her values in order to fit in. She's tempted to have a few

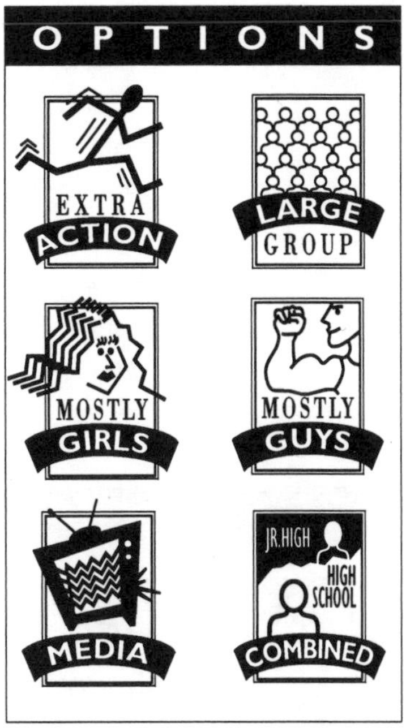

drinks so she can start enjoying herself.)

What are her options now? What might some of the consequences of these options be? (She could leave, though that might be very difficult. If she did, her friends might think she's a party pooper. She could give in and have a few drinks. This would be a violation of the law, since she's underage. She might end up feeling guilty about this, especially now that she's a Christian. She could stay and continue to feel miserable. She could tell her friends how she feels. They might understand, in which case Carla really could be a positive witness. On the other hand, they might laugh at her.)

What were some of Jerome's options before he agreed to Ken's plan? (He could tell Ken to forget it. He could agree to go along with it.)

What kinds of thoughts do you think are going through Jerome's mind the next day as Ken is coming through his lane? ("I shouldn't be doing this." "Good thing there's no one behind Ken." "I wonder if anyone is watching." "I wish I hadn't agreed to this." "Wow, we're gonna be rich!")

What are some of Jerome's options now? What might the consequences of each option be? (He could ask Ken to put the stuff back he's not willing to pay for. This might damage his friendship with Ken. He could go ahead with the plan. This could lead to his getting caught. He might get away with it, but then his conscience might bother him.)

In both cases, would you say the temptations were getting easier to resist, or harder to resist the further the person got into the situation? Why is this? Point out that temptation tends to have a spiraling effect. It's usually easier to resist early on. The more we give in to it, the harder it is to break the cycle. Ask for some examples of this dynamic in real life. Kids might mention things like drug abuse, alcohol, sexual promiscuity, and other bad habits.

Why are some temptations so hard to resist? (Often, the temptation promises some type of pleasure or satisfaction. It's hard to "deny ourselves." Sometimes we rationalize that it's really not so bad.)

Summarize: **I don't know about you, but for me, I've given in to temptation more than I care to admit. Sometimes temptation can seem impossible to resist, but God does provide ways for us to do just that. Today we're going to talk about how.**

STEP 3

The Great Escape

(Needed: Bibles, paper, pencils, chalkboard and chalk or newsprint and marker)

Say: **To give us some perspective, let's take a look at how well the Israelites—God's chosen people—handled some of the temptations they faced.**

Have someone read aloud I Corinthians 10:1-11. Then ask: **What kinds of temptations did the Israelites have trouble with?** (Worshiping idols, sexual immorality, grumbling.)

How are some of the temptations we face similar to those the Israelites faced? (Materialism—the desire for things—is kind of like worshiping idols. We are also tempted by sexual immorality. Like the Israelites, we are tempted to "grumble" when things don't go our way.)

Have someone read aloud I Corinthians 10:12, 13. Then ask: **Why is it important for us to know about other people who have fallen to temptation?** (Knowing about others who've fallen to temptation keeps us from getting overconfident in our ability to withstand temptation. In essence, God is saying, "If it can happen to them, it can happen to you.")

How does God "provide a way out" of temptations? (When we ask for His help, He will give us the strength to say no to tempting situations. He will also bring other Christians into our lives to encourage us to resist temptation.)

Explain: **We are in a constant battle against temptation. And a key to winning any battle is preparation. Just prior to the passages we've just looked at, Paul gives a prescription for being prepared for temptations. Let's take a look at that now.**

Have group members form teams of three or four. Distribute paper and pencils to each team. Instruct each team to read I Corinthians 9:24-27. Then write the following phrases on the board: "strict training," "crown that will last forever," "running aimlessly," and "beat my body and make it my slave." Instruct the teams to write down how each phrase might be a helpful reminder for us in our battle against temptation.

Give the teams a few minutes to work. When they're finished, have them share their responses. Use the following information to supple-

OPTIONS

ment the teams' answers.

• *Strict training*—We can't go into battle unprepared or untrained. Every day we must "train" by resisting one temptation at a time. The more we train, the better we will get at resisting tempting situations.

• *Crown that will last forever*—Giving in to temptation may mean immediate pleasure or benefits; however, doing things God's way—resisting temptation—yields everlasting benefits.

• *Running aimlessly*—If we know the kinds of temptations that are difficult for us to resist, we can prepare ourselves for them. If we don't prepare ourselves for them, we're "running aimlessly."

• *Beat my body and make it my slave*—Often, giving in to temptation is the result of not being able to control the urges of our bodies. If we learn to deny our sinful fleshly urges, we, in essence, "gain control" of our bodies.

Afterward, ask: **How can we really train or prepare to face temptation?** (We can think ahead about the temptations we might face and how we can be ready to resist them. We can plan words to say or actions to take in specific situations.)

Read aloud Matthew 4:1-11, which describes Jesus' temptation in the wilderness. Then ask: **What are some of the temptations Jesus faced here?** (Physical temptation to eat when He was very hungry; the temptation to prove who He was; the temptation to have a lot of power.)

How did Jesus fight these temptations? (In each instance, He quoted Scripture to Satan.)

STEP 4

Ready for Battle

(Needed: Index cards, Bibles, paper, pencils)

Have group members reassemble into the teams formed in Step 3. Give each team two index cards. The teams should write down two very tempting situations that kids their age often face. After all the teams have come up with two situations, have them switch cards with another team.

Instruct the teams to come up with at least two ideas for resisting each tempting situation described on the cards. At least one of the ideas should be something a person could do in preparation for the temptation before he or she has to face it.

Give the teams a few minutes to work. When they're finished, have them explain their ideas. After each team shares its ideas, ask for additional input from the rest of the group.

Afterward, explain: **We can face and resist temptation. Preparing for it definitely helps, but we can't do it alone. As the I Corinthians passage tells us, "God is faithful." He'll provide the way and the strength for us to resist temptation if we prepare ourselves as much as possible and rely on Him for help when temptation comes.**

STEP 5

Committed to Resist

Say: **We've come up with some ways to help us face temptations. But we shouldn't pretend that resisting temptation is easy. Sometimes it's very hard. We've mentioned some of the biggies, the ones that can be most damaging to our lives: sex, drinking, drugs, etc. Unfortunately, they're the biggies precisely because their appeal is so strong. Millions of kids—and adults—have fallen to each of these temptations. Maybe some of you have. But that doesn't mean you can't stop now and move on from here with a clean slate.**

What I'd like you to do now is between you and God. I'm not going to ask you to sign a card or tell a partner what you're going to do. But I want you to consider making a commitment to seek a way out when you face temptation.

Don't promise God that you'll never, ever give in to temptation. That kind of promise sets you up for failure. But promise Him that you'll prepare yourself by rehearsing some of the things we've talked about today that we can do to prepare for temptation. And promise Him that you'll try to lean on Him for help when tempting times come.

Give group members a few minutes of silence to make their own commitments to God. Then close your session with prayer.

OPTIONS

Holiness Quiz

Name ______________________

Date ______________________

Score ______________________

1. What are two motivations Christians have for resisting temptation?

____

____

2. Name three passages of Scripture that can be helpful to us when we face temptations.

____

____

____

3. According to Colossians 3:1-17, what should Christians concentrate on?

____

4. Name three things God has given us to help us determine what's right and what's wrong.

____

____

____

5. According to Galatians 5:16-26, what is the key principle for determining right and wrong?

____

____

____

Holiness Quiz

Answer Key

Name ______________________________

Date ______________________________

Score ______________________________

1. What are two motivations Christians have for resisting temptation?

   To avoid God's punishment

   To demonstrate our thankfulness to God for all that He's done for us

2. Name three passages of Scripture that can be helpful to us when we face temptations.

   Psalm 121

   II Corinthians 5:1-10

   II Corinthians 6:14–7:1

3. According to Colossians 3:1-17, what should Christians concentrate on?

   Things above

4. Name three things God has given us to help us determine what's right and what's wrong.

   The Bible

   The Holy Spirit

   Other Christians

5. According to Galatians 5:16-26, what is the key principle for determining right and wrong?

   If an action is done to satisfy the Holy Spirit, it is right. If an action is done to satisfy our sinful human nature, it is wrong.

How Tempting!

Read each of the following case studies and write down some of the person's options at each stage of the story.

1. Carla is a new Christian, but a lot of her friends don't know this yet. One of them, Keesha, invites Carla to a birthday party at a local club featuring male strippers. Carla's been to the club before and had a good time—maybe too good of a time, judging by the hangover she had the next day. Now she's not sure how to fit this in with her new faith. *Maybe I could go and not drink this time*, she reasons. *And I certainly don't need to stuff any money in anybody's shorts this time. Besides, maybe I can witness to my friends.* What are some of Carla's options?

Carla says she'll go. At the club, all of her friends are having a great time. But Carla's just not into it. Her friends tell her to loosen up. Carla knows that she'll fit in better if she has a few drinks. Her fake I.D. is still in her purse. What are her options now?

2. Jerome just got a part-time job as a cashier at the new discount store. Once in a while he's been tempted to take some merchandise home, but he fears he'd get caught. One day his best friend, Ken, hatches an idea for getting a lot of stuff really cheap. Ken will bring a bunch of expensive items through Jerome's lane. Jerome will ring some of them up (the less expensive ones) and not ring up the expensive ones. "No one'll know," Ken laughs. "Besides, that store makes so much money, they'll never miss it." What are some of Jerome's options?

Jerome says he'll do it, so long as Ken takes the heat if they get caught. The next day, Ken comes through the line with a cartful of electronic equipment and CDs. Luckily, there's no one else in line after Ken. What are Jerome's options now?

Extra Action

Step 2

Ask for four volunteers to roleplay the conversations between Carla and Keesha and Jerome and Ken. Briefly describe each situation and then let your actors carry on the dialogue. Interrupt the action and have the rest of the group members comment on Carla and Jerome's temptations, options, and consequences. If you want to get the entire group more actively involved, divide into teams of three or four and have each team develop its own skit in which someone starts off with a little temptation, but ends up in serious trouble. Give teams some time to develop their skits; then have them present the skits to the rest of the group. You could make into a more lighthearted activity if you have volunteers simply pantomime the characters' actions and have the rest of the group guess what is happening.

Step 3

Have group members form teams. Give each team a supply of cardboard, paper, scissors, tape, and assorted other items to make something that will remind them of the four phrases from I Corinthians 9:24-27 that you've written on the board. Coming up with something to depict the crown that lasts forever will be easy, but what will the teams create to depict strict training, running aimlessly, and "beat my body and make it my slave"? After giving some time for teams to develop their creations, have them share what they came up with and how the phrases might be helpful reminders to us in our battle against temptation. If your group is large, or if you have limited time, assign just one of the four phrases to each team.

Small Group

Step 3

Don't break into teams to discuss the I Corinthians 9:24-27 passage. Instead, make two columns on the board. Label them "Costs" and "Benefits." Have kids list the costs and benefits of the following:

• Strict training to be a better Christian.
• Resisting temptation. (If necessary, list specific types of temptations.)

When discussing the Matthew 4:1-11 passage, list the costs and benefits that Jesus might have given for resisting these temptations. Ask: **What did it cost Jesus not to follow Satan's advice? What was the benefit to Him, and to us?**

Step 4

As a group, compile a list of the top five temptations your group members and/or other kids their age face. Discuss some strategies for preparing for and resisting each of these temptations. Afterward, have each group member share about a time when he or she really felt tempted to do something—but didn't do it. Ask: **How hard was it for you to resist the temptation? Why didn't you give in to it? How did you feel at the time? How do you feel about it now?** Be prepared to share some of your own experiences, because this is an area where some kids may be reluctant to share very much. Perhaps in a smaller group setting, they will be more likely to open up.

Large Group

Step 1

This step may not work if you have a very large group of kids. If you don't think it will work with your group, try another activity. At the start of your meeting, have a big batch of popcorn on hand. Pass some out to each kid. Arrange in advance to have one kid throw a piece or two at someone else. After everyone has some popcorn, leave the room for a few minutes. Tell kids to "behave themselves" while you're gone. After you leave, your accomplice should throw some popcorn. See if he or she can tempt anyone else to join in a popcorn fight. When you come back, find out what happened. Were kids tempted to throw their popcorn or not? If so, why? If not, why not?

Step 2

Have kids form teams to discuss the two case studies on Repro Resource 9. If you have time, instruct each team to come up with an ending for each case study. After a few minutes, have each team share what it came up with. Then say: **Here's how the writer of this stuff says the cases turned out. Carla gave in and had a few drinks. That didn't really help her enjoy herself, because she felt kind of guilty. The next day, she asked God for forgiveness. A few days later, Keesha thanked Carla for her birthday gift, and asked if something was bothering Carla the night of the party. Carla told Keesha about her new faith, and eventually Keesha became a Christian too. As for Jerome, he told Ken to put the stuff back because he just couldn't go through with it. Ken was relieved, because he wasn't sure he wanted to go through with it either. After work, Jerome and Ken bumped into Carla and Keesha at the Burger Hut. They became great friends. Years later, Jerome married Carla, and Keesha married Ken. They all won Nobel Peace Prizes and lived happily ever after.**

Step 3
Tell your group members that it's their job to "teach" the rest of the session on resisting temptation. Write the Scripture passages (I Corinthians 9:24–10:13; Matthew 4:1-11) on the board. Instruct group members to come up with the following:

- at least five questions about the I Corinthians passage.
- at least three questions about the Matthew passage.

If you have eight or more kids, divide into at least two teams. Give one passage to each team to "teach" to the other. Give the teams at least ten minutes to prepare, and ten more minutes to teach. You might want to use some of the material from the session to supplement the discussion.

Step 5
If you think your kids won't respond well to a time of silence in which they make a commitment to God to seek a way out of tempting situations, you might want to consider something a little more directive. Give each kid a stamped envelope, some notepaper, and a pen. Have group members address their envelopes to themselves and write a letter to themselves with the following information:
"The next time I'm tempted to ____________________, I will seek God's help to resist it by ____________________. I know I'll be tempted again, so one way to prepare for it would be to ____________________."

If this format doesn't work, let kids express their thoughts in other ways. When they're finished writing, have them put the letters in the envelopes, seal them, and give them to you. You should mail them out in a couple of weeks.

Step 3
It's possible that parts of the I Corinthians passage will be difficult to grasp. Some of the language (like 10:2-4) is highly symbolic and may require a good deal of explanation. You might want to focus on four shorter passages:

- *Genesis 3:1-13.* Discuss how the serpent tempted Adam and Eve. Look for parallels in our own lives, especially in the ways they tried to justify what they had done.
- *I Corinthians 10:12, 13.* Discuss how to stand firm, how it feels to know everyone struggles with temptation, and the fact that God won't tempt (test) us beyond what we can bear.
- *Matthew 4:1-11.* Compare Jesus' temptation with Adam and Eve's and our own.
- *Hebrews 2:18.* Discuss how Jesus can help us fight temptation.

Step 4
This activity may be asking a bit much of those with little or no Bible background. As an alternative, ask two or three mature Christians to share with your group about their own methods for dealing with temptation. Set it up as a panel discussion, in which kids address questions and people on the panel take turns responding. Here are some questions you might want to ask:

- **Does temptation ever decrease or go away altogether if you fight it long enough?**
- **How do you resist temptation?**
- **Does it ever get easier to fight temptation?**
- **What Scripture verses do you rely on when you're tempted?**
- **When you give in to temptation, how do you feel, and what do you do about it?**

Step 1
Trying to "trick" your group into temptation might not be conducive to developing fellowship. If you'd rather spend the time in sharing, have each group member draw a picture of something he or she is tempted by. Let group members be as specific or as general as they wish. Some might simply draw a television if they are tempted to watch too much TV. Others might be more daring and draw a beer can, a member of the opposite sex, or some other specific object of temptation. Make sure you draw something yourself. After a few minutes, share your drawings with one another. In Step 4, you could use these drawings as the temptations for which you develop strategies for resisting. In Step 5, you could spend time in prayer, asking God to help you and your group members fight these temptations.

Step 5
If your group likes to sing, you might want to sing a chorus of commitment like "Lord, Be Glorified," "I'm Yours," or "King Jesus Is All" after your time of prayer. Whatever song you choose, discuss how it could help us resist temptation if we were to sing it to ourselves (or at least think of the words) during trying times. Challenge kids to learn the song well enough to be able to sing it from memory during a difficult time.

MOSTLY GIRLS

Step 2

Many of your group members may not be tempted by some of the "major" things we think of as temptations. Spend a few minutes discussing temptations that are more subtle, such as a hurting wisecrack that gets a laugh at someone else's expense or unhealthy thoughts or attitudes. Ask: **Why are some things tempting to you and not necessarily to another person? Could one temptation be "major" for one person and "minor" for another? How does God judge our temptations?**

Step 4

After the index cards have been exchanged, have the teams use a comic-strip format to present ideas for resisting their assigned temptations. Distribute strips of paper and markers. Suggest that the teams use at least four different "panels" to present their ideas. After a few minutes, have each team share its comic strip with the rest of the group.

MOSTLY GUYS

Step 2

Skip the case study about Carla on Repro Resource 9. Instead, use this one: **Carlos is on the track team at school. Some of the other guys are using steroids and are getting stronger. Carlos knows he shouldn't take steroids, but he wouldn't mind being stronger himself. Besides, if his performance in track would improve, he might be able to get a full scholarship to college. One day in the locker room, Carlos's friend, Steve, offers to get Carlos some "juice." "All the guys are doing it," Steve says. "Besides, it won't really hurt you if you're only on it for short periods of time." What are some of Carlos's options? Carlos agrees to try it. He's amazed at the results. He gains about fifteen pounds in a few short months. Carlos is hooked. Now he wants to get even bigger. He figures a little more acne and some aggressiveness is a small price to pay for a full scholarship. Carlos's parents notice the change, and they confront him about it. What are his options now?**

Step 4

If you want to focus in on sexual temptation, have your guys compare and contrast Joseph's experience with David's. Joseph's experience with Potiphar's wife is in Genesis 39. David's experience with Bathsheba is in II Samuel 11. Note the downward progression of David's sin. First he has idle time, then he sees Bathsheba, then he sends someone to find out about her, then he sleeps with her, then she gets pregnant, etc. Discuss how David could have resisted at each step, and how it became more difficult to resist as he got further into the situation. Contrast this with Joseph's integrity. Note that in the short term, at least, Joseph's decision to resist temptation cost him dearly. But, in the long run, the benefits of resisting far outweighed the consequences.

EXTRA FUN

Step 1

Develop the entire session around a domino theme. Depending on the size of your group, you'll need a large supply of dominoes. Have group members form teams. Give each team several dominoes. Have a contest to see which team can build the most elaborate lineup—the type in which one domino knocks over the next one, and so on. Set a time limit for each team. At your signal, each team should knock over its first domino. Pay attention to which team's sequence lasts the longest. Tie this in to the "domino effect of temptation," noting how one temptation tends to lead to another, which leads to another. Later in your session, you can play other domino games (building the tallest tower in two minutes, tossing the most dominoes in a bucket from ten feet away, etc.). You could even play actual dominoes, if anyone knows how. To top it all off, have some Domino's pizza delivered!

Step 5

The session closes on a serious note, so here's something you could try after the session is over to liven things up a bit. It loosely ties in to the subject of temptation. Play your own version of the popular game "Taboo." Divide into two teams. Each team should come up with at least ten words that the other team will try to guess, and five "taboo" words that the other team's clue-giver can't say. (For example: You might try to get the team to guess the words "King David" without saying Goliath, Psalms, Jonathan, Bathsheba, or shepherd. Obviously, the words King and David can't be used either.) Have teams write down each word to be guessed (as well its accompanying "taboo" words) on separate slips of paper. Elect a clue-giver from each team to see how many of the words he or she can get the rest of the team to guess in one minute. If a "taboo" word is said, the other team gets the point. If a word is guessed, the team keeps the point. Play several rounds.

MEDIA

Step 1
Before anyone else arrives, hide a video camera somewhere in the room to capture what happens after you leave to "fetch" the candy bars. Make sure the video is well concealed and that it's focused on where the action will take place. If you don't want to use anyone as an accomplice, you could simply leave your answer key in plain sight when you leave. When you come back, go over the quiz answers and then announce that you're going to show an episode of "Totally Hidden Video"! Review the video and see what happens. Point out that God doesn't need video cameras to know what we're up to!

Step 2
Have group members form two teams—guys on one team and girls on the other. Give each team a copy of Repro Resource 9, a cassette player that records, and a blank tape. Have the girls record some dialogue between Carla and Keesha and between Carla and her friends at the club. Have the guys record the conversation between Jerome and Ken. Both teams should feel free to introduce new characters, add narration, sound effects, commercial breaks—whatever. Give the teams several minutes to work. When they're finished, have each team share its tape with the other.

SHORT MEETING TIME

Step 1
The whole tempting setup might take more time than you have. If this is the case, start off your session by serving some really salty food—pretzels, chips, popcorn—the saltier the better. After kids have eaten a bunch, pour yourself a big glass of water (or any other refreshing beverage). Let them know you're really enjoying this. Describe how great it tastes after all the salty food. Then tell your kids that they can't have any, because they aren't old enough yet. Let them talk about how that makes them feel. Explain that this is a bit like fighting temptation. Often society parades very tempting things before our eyes, but then the church says "Don't." Ask: **Why is this? How does it make you feel? When is it hardest for you to resist temptation?**

Step 4
Instead of having teams come up with tempting situations, assign one of the following general temptations to each team:

- temptation to have sex before marriage
- temptation to drink alcoholic beverages
- temptation to skip church activities
- temptation to buy more than you need.

Explain that each team should develop a plan for resisting its assigned temptation. Point out that we need to think through our strategies before we find ourselves in a tempting situation. Suggest that even if we've given in to some of these temptations in the past, that's no reason why we can't fight them in the future.

URBAN

Step 3
Have group members form teams of three. As you read the following scenario, team members should pretend that they are friends of Miguel, the person in the scenario. They should come up with strategies for dealing with the situation. The scenario is as follows:
Miguel has been getting bullied around by Rafael, the leader of the Overlords gang. For the past two days on the way home from school, Rafael has threatened Miguel at knife point, forcing him to do some humiliating things. Miguel knows that if he resists or tries to stand up to Rafael, he'll get stabbed. Rafael has already stabbed at least fourteen people, killing one of them. Miguel is getting desperate. He's tempted to do something crazy. What would you advise him to do? Give the teams a few minutes to respond. Then continue with the story. **The strategy you suggested didn't work. Now the members of the Overlords are mad. They've put the word out that they're going to get Miguel one way or another. Miguel is so scared and confused that he's tempted to commit suicide. To him, killing himself would be better than always having to look over his shoulder. Miguel has a bottle of sleeping pills that he's planning to take to end his life. He says he can see no good reason to live. What reasons can you give him? What advice can you offer him for his problem with the Overlords?** Give teams a few minutes to respond.

Step 4
Offer some suggestions to get kids thinking about the temptations they face in the city. For example, you might suggest things like "making money as a sentry (or lookout) for a drug dealer" or "buying stolen goods from someone on the street."

Jr. High / High School Combined

Step 2

The case studies on Repro Resource 9 may not be applicable to junior highers. You might want to consider using the following one instead: **Chad and Dustin are good friends—that is, until Dustin goes to an amusement park with a couple of other guys and doesn't invite Chad to go along. Chad thinks of a way to get back at Dustin. One time Dustin got really drunk when his parents were out of town. Dustin's parents never found out about it. When Dustin told Chad about the experience, he begged Chad never to tell anyone else about it. Chad swore he'd never tell. Now he's tempted to call a mutual friend, Marty, and blab all about it. What are some of Chad's options? Chad calls Marty and tells him all about the time Dustin got drunk. A few days later, Dustin asks Chad if he broke his promise. Somehow, Dustin's parents found out about the incident. Now Dustin is grounded for a month. What are Chad's options now?**

Step 4

Rather than having your junior highers come up with tempting situations on their own, you might want to give them the following situations to discuss:

- **You have a clear view of the smart kid's test paper. You're tempted to cheat.**
- **You broke a vase that your mother really liked. You're tempted to lie about it.**
- **At a party, some friends offer you a beer. They'll laugh at you if you don't drink it.**
- **You're at a friend's house, and he or she is going to watch a video that your dad said you were too young to see. You're tempted to watch it because your dad will never know.**

Extra Challenge

Step 3

The I Corinthians 10:1-13 passage makes several references to Old Testament history. Spend some time looking up the passages in which these events occurred. Here are some references you could look up. (How many of these can your kids find on their own?)

- "under the cloud"—Exodus 13:21, 22; Numbers 9:15-23; 14:14; Deuteronomy 1:33
- "passed through the sea"—Exodus 14:15-31
- "baptized into Moses"—Exodus 14:31
- "spiritual food/drink"—Exodus 16:2-36; 17:1-7
- "God was not pleased"—Numbers 14:22-24, 28-35
- "idolaters"—Exodus 32:1-6
- "in one day twenty-three thousand of them died"—Numbers 25:9
- "do not grumble, as some of them did"—Numbers 16:41.

Ask: **Do you think the Israelites were dense for not following God after seeeing His great power? Are we ever guilty of the same thing?**

Step 4

In addition to coming up with ways to prepare for and resist the temptations listed on the cards, have each team come up with one or two Scripture verses that would help someone out of the tempting situation. This would be a good opportunity to stress the importance of memorizing Scripture. Point out that Jesus made good use of Scripture when Satan tempted Him. Have kids share some of the verses they've memorized, and discuss some techniques that help with Bible memorization. Some suggestions might include learning the verses as songs, writing them down and displaying them in prominent places, etc.

Planning Checklist

Date Used:

Approx. Time

Step 1: Tempting Setup ______
o Large Group
o Fellowship & Worship
o Extra Fun
o Media
o Short Meeting Time
Things needed:

Step 2: Tantalizing Temptations ______
o Extra Action
o Large Group
o Mostly Girls
o Mostly Guys
o Media
o Combined Junior High/High School
Things needed:

Step 3: The Great Escape ______
o Extra Action
o Small Group
o Heard It All Before
o Little Bible Background
o Urban
o Extra Challenge
Things needed:

Step 4: Ready for Battle ______
o Small Group
o Little Bible Background
o Mostly Girls
o Mostly Guys
o Short Meeting Time
o Urban
o Combined Junior High/High School
o Extra Challenge
Things needed:

Step 5: Committed to Resist ______
o Heard It All Before
o Fellowship & Worship
o Extra Fun
Things needed:

SESSION

5 Fighting for Right

YOUR GOALS FOR THIS SESSION:

Choose one or more

- [ ] To help kids recognize that it's sometimes necessary to stand up and take action for our faith.
- [ ] To help kids understand that injustice is not just something that happens on a global level.
- [ ] To help kids begin to fight unjust attitudes within themselves as well as injustice they see around them.
- [ ] Other ______________________________

Your Bible Base:

Isaiah 58:3-11
Amos 8:4-7
Micah 6:6-8

STEP 1

Musical Chaos

(Needed: An instrument or something to produce music, chairs, container, items for the game)

OPTIONS

Open the session with a game of "musical chaos." This game is a variation of musical chairs. Form a circle of chairs, backs toward the center, with one chair for each group member. Place the chairs about eight inches apart, so that there's just enough room for a person to squeeze between them. On the floor in the center of the circle, place a container with one fewer item in it than you have participants. Use most anything you have available for the items, but make sure they don't have sharp points. You could use marbles, cards, crayons, game pieces, dry beans, etc. [NOTE: Any breakable or tearable items will likely get broken or torn during this game.]

Have everyone take a seat in the circle. Then start playing some music. When the music stops, everyone is to jump up, squeeze between the chairs, and try to grab one of the items in the container.

The person who doesn't get an item is eliminated from the round, just like in musical chairs. After each round, remove one chair from the circle and one item from the container.

Continue playing until only one person remains. Declare him or her the winner.

Afterward, ask: **How is the game we just played similar to living the Christian life?** Group members will probably ask for more specifics before they answer. Don't give them any. Leave the question as wide open as possible. Encourage them to use some creativity and humor in coming up with their answers.

If no one mentions it, suggest that in the Christian life—just like in the game—there's a time to "sit around" (attending church, listening to music, reading the Bible, etc.) and a time to stand up and take action. There's more to being holy than studying the Bible, praying, and resisting temptation. It also involves taking action on those things God wants us to act on. Today's session deals with those things.

STEP
2

A Need to Stand

(Needed: Copies of Repro Resource 10, pencils)

Distribute copies of "The Way It Should Be" (Repro Resource 10) and pencils. Instruct group members to read through the situations on the sheet and write down what they'd like to have happen in each situation. Group members should work individually on the sheets.

Give group members a few minutes to complete the assignment. When everyone is finished, go over the situations one at a time. Make sure you get responses from several group members for each situation.

Ask: **What were you hoping would happen in these situations?** (For some of the situations, group members may have hoped that justice would be done. For some of the situations, group members may have hoped that mercy would be shown to them or their families. For some of the situations, group members may have hoped for help from someone else.)

What common theme do you see among the four situations on the sheet? (In order to resolve each situation, someone would have to stand up and do what's right. For the first situation, it would have to be the thief or someone who witnessed the theft. For the second situation, it would have to be someone who could help the family financially. For the third situation, it would have to be the person who actually cheated. For the fourth situation, it would have to be the friend who may know something.)

Have you or anyone you know ever faced a situation in which you were dependent on someone else standing up and doing what's right? If so, tell us about it. You may want to be prepared with an example of your own to get things going. Encourage several group members to tell their stories. After each one, briefly discuss what the consequences might have been if the person hadn't acted.

Then ask: **Have you or anyone you know ever been the one who stood up for what's right to help someone else in need?** Encourage group members to respond, even if it means "bragging on themselves" a little. Ask volunteers to describe how they felt about standing up for what's right. Were they nervous? Did they feel outnumbered? Were they proud? Were they sorry? Would they do it again?

OPTIONS

STEP 3

The Just and the Unjust

(Needed: Bibles, paper, pencils, chalkboard and chalk or newsprint and marker)

OPTIONS

Say: **Let's take a look at some principles in Scripture that encourage us to stand up for what's right.**

Have group members form two teams. Distribute paper and pencils to each team. Then write the following questions on the board: "What is justice?" and "What is injustice?" Assign one of the questions to each team.

Have the "justice" team look up Isaiah 58:3-11. Have the "injustice" team look up Amos 8:4-7. Instruct each team to read its assigned passage and answer its assigned question, based on the passage. Encourage team members to think about what the passages mean and not just copy down the words they find there.

Give the teams a few minutes to work. When they're finished, have each one share its definition. Write down key parts of their answers on the board. Use the following suggestions to supplement the teams' responses.

What is justice? (Justice is freeing the oppressed, sharing food with the hungry, providing shelter for the homeless, clothing the naked, and not turning away from those who need you.)

What is injustice? (Injustice is trampling and cheating the needy and "doing away" with the poor in our efforts to get ahead in life.)

Then ask: **How do these definitions of justice and injustice make you feel?** (Some group members may feel guilty because they're not doing enough to rid their own lives of injustice toward the poor and needy. Others may see justice and injustice as being measured on a large scale, and not a personal one; so they may not feel affected by these definitions.)

How does fighting against injustice or fighting for justice fit into our faith as Christians? (God wants us to care about other people's needs. He wants us to fight for others' rights, not just our own. In Mark 12:31, Jesus says that one of the two most important commandments is "Love your neighbor as yourself.")

Say: **There's one more passage from a minor prophet that outlines specifically what God expects from us in this area of justice and injustice.**

Have someone read aloud Micah 6:6-8. Then ask: **How do justice**

and mercy fit together? (We should act justly ourselves, and love mercy. If we love mercy, we'll certainly show it to others. Having mercy on others makes us want justice for them.)

How does humility fit into the picture of justice and mercy? (We shouldn't want things solely for ourselves—including recognition for showing justice and mercy to others. Our primary concern and motivation should be the needs of others.)

What does walking with God have to do with all this? (When we walk with God and stay close to Him, He helps us do what's right and gives us the right attitudes toward others.)

Say: **God does want us to stand up for what's right. Sometimes that involves justice; other times it involves having mercy.**

STEP 4

What Can We Do?

(Needed: Chalkboard and chalk or newsprint and marker)

Ask: **Who are the "oppressed" in our society today?** (Poor people, minorities, unpopular kids, people in Third World countries, etc.)

Say: **When we talk about injustice, sometimes it seems so widespread that no individual or group could do anything to combat it. But even though we may not be able to change all of the world's injustice, we certainly can change unjust attitudes within ourselves—as well as some of the injustices we see around us.**

Have group members look back at the lists you made on the board in defining justice and injustice. Then have them brainstorm a new list, this time of injustices they've seen in their schools and your community. Write their ideas on the board next to the previous list.

Use the following suggestions to supplement the group's list: racism, hungry children, innocent kids getting punished, bad treatment of kids who aren't popular, elderly people unable to take care of their homes, unborn children being aborted, divorced moms struggling to make ends meet, etc.

After group members have come up with a list of ten or more injustices, discuss which of the injustices your group could affect. Examine ways your group members could work together to combat injustices.

OPTIONS

For instance, you might plan a special activity (such as a game night or a concert), and have your group members make a point of inviting kids they've never talked to before (the "unpopular" kids in school). Or you might organize a volunteer baby-sitting service through your church for single working mothers struggling to make ends meet.

If you have time, spend about ten minutes planning what you're going to do. Zero in on one specific activity. Assign group members different tasks in organizing the operation. Then schedule additional meetings to hammer out details.

STEP 5

Even You Can Prevent Injustice!

OPTIONS

Say: **We've come up with a way our group can work to lessen the injustice around us. Whatever we can do as a group is a good start, but it's not enough. We also need to work individually to combat the injustices around us. Let's take a look at what we can do as individuals the rest of the time.**

Have group members form teams of three or four. Within their teams, group members should brainstorm ways they, as individuals, could help prevent injustice in their lives and in society around them.

If group members have trouble coming up with ideas, suggest things like "I could make plans to have lunch with someone at school who doesn't seem to have any friends"; "I could secretly give some of my not-too-out-of-style clothes to someone who really needs them"; or "I could stand up for kids who get criticized at school because of their faith."

After each person has suggested at least a couple of ideas, say: **Now take a minute to think about the suggestions your team has come up with. Decide which one or ones you really want to work on and tell your team how you're going to do it.**

After group members have discussed with their teams what they're going to do, say: **We've mentioned before that one way to fight temptation is through the support of Christian friends. The same principle applies to helping one another stand up and do what's right.**

Encourage team members to call each other sometime during the week to see how the injustice fighting is going. If group members would feel comfortable praying together in their teams, have them do so.

Wrap up this session with the following blessing from Isaiah 58:9-11: **"If you do away with the yoke of oppression, with the pointing finger and malicious talk, and if you spend yourselves in behalf of the hungry and satisfy the needs of the oppressed, then your light will rise in the darkness, and your night will become like the noonday. The Lord will guide you always; he will satisfy your needs in a sun-scorched land and will strengthen your frame. You will be like a well-watered garden, like a spring whose waters never fail."**

STEP 6

Holy Wrap-Up

(Needed: Copies of Repro Resource 11, pencils)

This step is designed to bring some closure to this course on personal holiness. Distribute copies of "Scrambled Holiness" (Repro Resource 11). If there's time during the session, have group members solve the puzzle. Then review some of the key concepts from the course. If there isn't time, hand the sheets out at the end of the session and go over them the next time you meet.

The number of each question corresponds to the session number that concept is from. Review key concepts as you go along. The answers are as follows:

(1) things above (Colossians 3:1-17)
(2) sinful human nature (Galatians 5:16-26)
(3) avoid punishment; gratitude (II Corinthians 5:1-10; 6:14–7:1)
(4) resist (I Corinthians 9:24–10:13)
(5) injustice (Isaiah 58:6-11)
Bonus question—Be separate (II Corinthians 6:17)

Emphasize that the bottom line is that God sets us apart to be holy. Our attitudes and actions will reflect this. Read aloud II Corinthians 7:1 as a final charge to your group members to live holy lives.

OPTIONS

THE WAY IT SHOULD BE

For each of the following situations, write a couple of sentences describing what you would like to see happen.

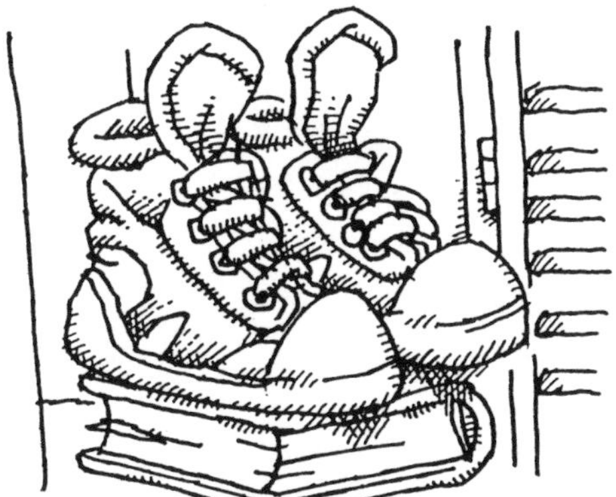

1. Someone else's stolen $100 basketball shoes were found in your locker. As a result, you've been suspended from the team until the matter is straightened out.
What do you want to happen?

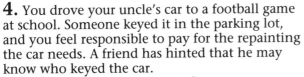

2. Your dad lost his job two months ago because of cutbacks where he worked. Your mom has been unable to work full time because she's recovering from major surgery. The hospital bill isn't completely paid, and the house payment is a month late. The electric company is threatening to turn off your electricity.
What do you want to happen?

3. A teacher is accusing you of cheating because several paragraphs of your research paper are the same as another student's. You did your paper on a computer at school, and are suspicious that the other person copied your files without your knowing it.
What do you want to happen?

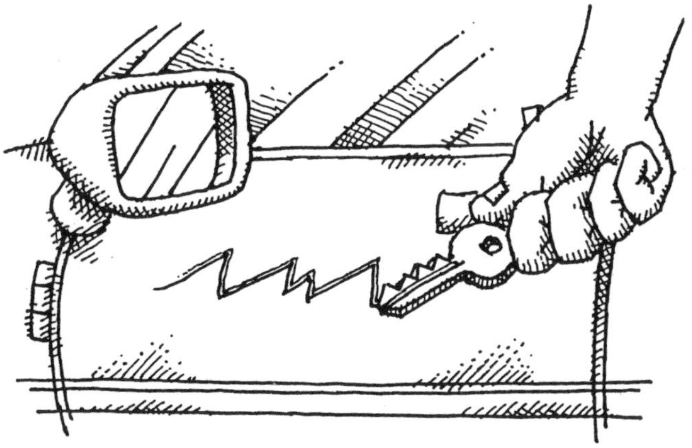

4. You drove your uncle's car to a football game at school. Someone keyed it in the parking lot, and you feel responsible to pay for the repainting the car needs. A friend has hinted that he may know who keyed the car.
What do you want to happen?

Scrambled Holiness

Unscramble the words below to find out what each sentence is saying.

1. In order to be holy, we should set our hearts and minds on

_ _ _ _ _ _ _ (◯) _ _ (◯).

N S I G H T B O E V A

2. When choosing between right and wrong, holy people seek to satisfy the Holy Spirit, not their

(◯) _ _ _ _ _ _ _ _ (◯) _

F U N I L S M U N H A

_ _ _ _ _ (◯).

A T R U N E

3. Two primary motivations for resisting temptation are to

(◯) _ _ _ _ (◯) _ _ _ _ _ _ _ _ _

D A V I O M E N S H I P N U T

and to show _ (◯) _ _ _ _ _ _ _ to God.

D R A G T U T I E

4. God always provides a way for us to

_ _ _ _ _ (◯) temptation.

S I S T E R

5. Another mark of a holy person is that he or she takes action to fight

_ _ _ _ _ _ _ _ (◯).

T I N J U I C E S

Bonus Question:
(Unscramble all the circled letters.)
Being holy means that God has called us to

_ _ _ _ _ _ _ _ _ _ _

from the rest of the crowd. (See II Corinthians 6:17.)

EXTRA ACTION

Step 2

Hold a brief courtroom trial for each of the four cases listed on Repro Resource 10. You can serve as Judge Whopper. Assign various roles.

Case #1: Defendant—the person with the locker in which the shoes were found; Plaintiff—the person who owns the shoes; attorneys on both sides.

Case #2: Plaintiff—the person taking the electric company to court for being so cruel; Defendant—an official of the electric company; attorneys for both sides.

Case #3: Defendant—the kid accused of cheating; Plaintiff—teacher; Witness—the other student; attorneys for both sides.

Case #4: Defendant—the kid who borrowed the car; Plaintiff—the uncle, who's decided to sue for damages; Witness—the friend who may know something; attorneys for both sides.

If you don't have time for all four cases, choose one or two to try. Give each side a minute or two to present its case. As judge, you should keep asking, **What is it that you want to see happen?** Let any remaining group members be the jury and decide the outcome of each case.

Step 6

Instead of having kids work on Repro Resource 11 individually, have them complete the sheet in teams of three or four. See which team can finish it correctly in the least amount of time. Afterward, explain that the winning team gets to choose the game your group will play to close out the session (and the series). The winning team may choose any game it likes—provided you have the equipment. However, explain that at various points of the game, you will "freeze" the action. When you do, everyone must stand perfectly still. You will ask someone what he or she learned about holiness during this series. After he or she answers, the game will continue as before. Freeze the game at least two or three times.

SMALL GROUP

Step 1

If your group is small, the musical chaos activity might not work very well. You can get the same point across if you're willing to work a little in advance. Before anyone arrives, move all the chairs out of the room. If you have really large chairs or couches, turn them over, or do something to them (remove cushions, place things on them, etc.) so that no one will be able to sit down. When kids arrive, they'll probably be curious about what's going on. See if anyone can guess. Unless they've read this ahead of time (which is highly unlikely), they won't have a clue. Say: **For the last few weeks, we've been sitting around and learning about what it means to be holy. Well, sometimes being holy requires that we get off our duffs and take action. That's what we're going to talk about today.** If the word "duffs" is offensive, forget you saw it here and substitute a word of your own choosing! (If you're really offended by it, write us a letter.)

Step 5

Instead of breaking into teams to brainstorm ways that individuals can fight injustice, stay together as one group. On the board (or a large sheet of paper), write all the letters of the alphabet. See if your group can list something an individual can do to fight injustice that starts with each letter. "A" could stand for "Arrange to have lunch with someone at school who doesn't have any friends." "B" could stand for "Buy some food and give it to the food pantry." Be flexible for some of the more difficult letters like *x* and *q*. "X" could be to "eXamine the newspaper more closely to learn about what's happening in the world." After compiling a list, have each group member choose one thing on the list to do this week.

LARGE GROUP

Step 1

If you want to eliminate kids faster from the musical chaos game, add a further dimension to it—a three-legged race. Have kids pair up and tie their legs together as in a three-legged race. (You'll lessen the chance of twisted ankles if you have them tie their legs together above the knee as well as at the ankle.) Follow the rules as described in the session. Have partners sit in two adjacent chairs. This might get a little frenzied, so discontinue the game if it looks as if someone might get hurt. You don't need to eliminate all of the teams in order to get your point across.

Step 3

If you want to have more than two teams looking up passages, here are some other passages about justice and injustice that you could assign:

- Isaiah 32:1-16
- Isaiah 42:1-7
- Isaiah 59:1-16
- Amos 5:6-24
- Micah 3:5-12

These are not easy passages, and should raise a lot of questions. Group members looking up these passages should simply look for examples of what injustice is or what justice is. What they discover should complement the definitions that are developed from the Isaiah 58:3-11 and Amos 8:4-7 passages.

Step 3
Even kids who think they've heard it all before probably won't be very familiar with the Isaiah and Amos passages chosen for this session. Both passages speak of things that aren't valued very highly today. The Isaiah passage speaks of fasting. Ask kids what they think of fasting. Ask: **Why don't more people fast today? What value is there in it? Is this passage saying that there's no real value in fasting?** Challenge your group members to a twelve- or twenty-four-hour fast. The Amos passage speaks of the New Moon and sabbath. Do your kids know what this is referring to? Have them look up Numbers 28:9-15. Commerce was forbidden during the New Moon festival and the sabbath. How do your kids view their "sabbaths?" Do they treat them as anything special? Challenge them to spend at least one entire Sunday this month in worship, rest, and relaxation—with no commerce.

Step 6
Arrange to have your group members summarize what they've learned in this course with a group of junior highers or adults. The presentation should be five to ten minutes long. Spend some time discussing how you want to communicate what you've learned, and make sure everyone in the group plays a part in pulling it off. Here are some ideas for how your presentation could be structured:
• Top ten things we learned about being holy
• What holiness is and isn't
• Questions and answers about holiness
• A news report about recent discoveries in holiness
• A video presentation called "Holiness Today"
• An interview with Internally and Externally Holy Joe (from Session 1)

Step 3
Those without much familiarity with the Bible may never have ventured near the prophets, especially the minor ones. Make sure you help them find Isaiah, Amos, and Micah in their Bibles. A little background on these prophets might be helpful. Supplement what's printed here with stuff you dig up on your own. Isaiah, Amos, and Micah all lived at roughly the same time (around 740 B.C.). Isaiah's name means "the Lord saves." Jewish tradition holds that he was sawed in half. The Book of Isaiah has many references to the Messiah (Jesus). Amos was a shepherd by profession. His book is all about social justice. Amos 5:24 captures his message very well. We don't know very much about Micah. Some say his book is a bit "schizophrenic" because it keeps bouncing back and forth between God's judgment and His deliverance—doom and hope.

Step 5
Sometimes those of us who write youth curriculum do you, the youth leader, a terrible disservice by assuming that you can always wrap each session up into a tidy package and that your kids will all make commitments that they will follow through on. You know better than anyone that your kids are still in-process, not finished products. If you sense your kids aren't ready to make any great commitments to fight injustice, don't push it. Feel free to skip this step altogether. Or simply have group members respond to this statement: **Someone once said, "Let my heart be broken with the things that break the heart of God." What do you think are some of the things that "break" God's heart? What are some things that break your heart?"** Talk about ways we can be more sensitive to people's needs, especially people who are victims of injustice. Point out that God will reward even the smallest steps we take in obedience to His Word.

Step 5
It's easy to lose sight of God's sovereignty and become overwhelmed by all the problems and injustices in the world. If you sense your kids are feeling this way, you might want to focus on Psalms 9 and 94 instead of, or in addition to, the Isaiah 58:9-11 passage. Have kids look at both of these psalms silently and, after a few minutes, read verses out loud (in no particular order) that are meaningful to them. After your time of prayer, sing Micah 6:8 ("He has shown thee, O man, what is good and what the Lord requires of thee. . . .") if you know it, or some other chorus. "Shine, Jesus, Shine" would be another fitting song to sing.

Step 6
Instead of taking time during the session to complete Repro Resource 11, give it to group members to take home. They should be able to solve it without looking in the leader's guide for the answers! Review the course by asking some questions that call for personal reflection:
• **What do you think it means to be holy?**
• **What is one thing you've learned that will help you live a holier life?**
• **What are the biggest obstacles to holiness that you are facing?**
• **What progress have you made in living a holy life?**

MOSTLY GIRLS

Step 2
After your group members have written down some responses to "The Way It Should Be" (Repro Resource 10), choose one or two of the situations to dramatize. Have group members form teams with enough people that they can ad-lib a possible solution to the situations you've chosen. Have each team set up the event and continue a dialogue or description of what could happen. Then use the discussion questions already provided.

Step 5
As a part of the discussion about injustice around us, ask your group members to discuss with their teams any injustices *they* may have experienced. Ask: **How did you react? What more** (or **else**) **could you have done in that situation? How can your personal experiences help us figure out what to do to help prevent injustice in our immediate world?**

MOSTLY GUYS

Step 1
Depending on your group, you might want to substitute another activity for the musical chaos game. Before the session, collect at least six empty two-liter bottles and their caps. Colored plastic bottles will work better than clear ones. Fill half of the bottles with water, and leave the other ones empty. Put the bottles in two groupings on a table at the far end of the room. To start the session, have group members form teams. Each team should have a supply of soft foam rubber balls (racquetballs might also work). The object is for each team to knock over all of its bottles with the fewest throws. One team will be throwing at empty bottles, and the other at full ones (though they won't know this at the start). It shouldn't take long before the team with full bottles cries "foul" and complains that the contest isn't fair. Use this to introduce the concept of injustice.

Step 2
Some guys may have difficulty coming up with answers to the questions you're supposed to ask after going over the situations on Repro Resource 10. Instead of focusing on your group members' personal experiences, try asking them to rate how difficult it would be (on a scale of 1 to 10, with 10 being the highest) to stand up for the following individuals:

• a skinny kid from church who's getting teased by some guys twice his size during gym.
• a skinny kid who people suspect might be gay who's being teased during gym.
• a kid who had his car vandalized (you know the guys who did it).
• a kid who's in a gang who had his car vandalized (you know the guys who did it).

Discuss the risks and rewards of standing up for each of these individuals.

EXTRA FUN

Step 1
Structure your whole session around a courtroom theme. Here are some ideas you might consider: come dressed as a judge; set up your room to resemble a courtroom; serve miniature gavels (marshmallows with pretzel sticks stuck in them); play some music from *L.A. Law* or *Perry Mason*; watch a segment from *The People's Court*, or a courtroom drama. To tie in to the topic of injustice, handcuff or put a ball and chain on all of your blue-eyed group members (or some other arbitrary physical characteristic). Make life difficult for these people. Don't let them have snacks, etc. Don't tell why you've zeroed in on this particular group. Let them experience (in a very small way) how it feels to be discriminated against.

Step 6
At the conclusion of your study of personal holiness, have everyone make a halo. You could use wire, aluminum foil, pipe cleaners, coat hangers—whatever you think will work. Have group members put on their halos; then take some group photos. An instant camera might work best. Display your photos in a prominent place so those outside your group can see how "holy" you've all become. After getting some laughs over the halos, remind kids that holiness is really an internal thing, not an external thing. God isn't impressed with our halos, but He does care a great deal about our hearts! Have everyone take off his or her halo and contribute it to some sort of group sculpture. Take a picture of this to display next to your halo photos.

MEDIA

Step 1
If you have time before or during the session, and you have access to several video cameras, try the following activity in place of the musical chaos game. Have group members form teams. Give each team a video camera. Take the teams to a public place to record several "person on the street" interviews. Give each team a different question to ask. Explain that the teams should ask their questions to a wide variety of people, not just teens or not just Christians. Here are some questions you could use:
• What does it mean to be holy?
• What is justice?
• Why is there so much injustice in the world?

It's probably best to send an adult helper with each team. Have your group members explain to people why they're interested in their comments—that it's a project for the church youth group. Instruct group members to be courteous, and thank those who take the time to respond. When you meet back together, have each team share its tape.

Step 4
Before discussing specific ways to fight injustice, show a video clip or listen to an audio tape of Dr. Martin Luther King (or any other public person) talk about injustice. You might want to check at your public library to see what they would suggest. You might also want to consider playing some reggae music, or other international music that speaks of social injustice. Again, your library might be a good source for this. Analyze the lyrics, looking for signs of anger, despair, and hope.

SHORT MEETING TIME

Step 1
The musical chaos game might be a lot of fun, but it might not be practical given your limited time—especially considering the rather loose connection it has to the topic of this session. Here's another way to make an equally tenuous connection to the topic—in one-tenth the time! Have everyone stand up. At your signal, group members should stand on one leg with their eyes closed. See who can stand the longest. For most people, it's pretty difficult to stay still. Instead of having your kids try to guess why you subjected them to this, say: **Part of what it means to be holy is to stand up and take action when we see things around us that aren't right. But we'll never take action if we keep our eyes closed, or ignore the injustice that's so visible all around us.**

Step 5
This entire step could be combined with Step 4. Have half of your group members think about things your group could do to get involved in the fight against injustice. Have the other half of your group members come up with a list of things individuals could do. After a few minutes, have each group share its ideas with the other. Then, as a group, decide on one project you're willing to tackle at this time. Set another time to discuss the details of the project. Then give kids a few minutes to think about specific things they're willing to commit to, to fight injustice as individuals.

URBAN

Step 2
You might want to consider adding the following situations to Repro Resource 10.
• You're walking home after dark from a friend's party when you notice a police car slowly passing you. Suddenly it turns around and heads straight for you. The lights and siren come on, and another police car screeches to a halt behind you. The cars corner you with their high beams. Two officers jump out with guns drawn and yell, "On the ground, Babyface!" You try to tell them you're not Babyface, but they won't listen. They pin you to the ground, handcuff you, and tell you you're under arrest for burglary. Then they whisk you away to the police station. What do you want to happen?
• Your eight-year-old brother comes home from school looking drugged. You ask what's wrong, and he says with slurred speech and uncontrollable laughter, "Nothing. I just feel happy!" You notice a sticker tattoo on his hand. He tells you a nice man gave it to him after school. It's an LSD sticker. What do you want to happen?

Step 4
Remind your group members that injustice is rarely changed by lethargy. Give them eight controversies—abortion, the death penalty, nuclear war, police abuse, drug crimes, poverty, homelessness, and the environment—to discuss and formulate opinions on. Encourage your group members to share their opinions and strategies not only with each other, but with people in the community. Point out that Christians making a stand for Jesus can accomplish great things in society.

JR. HIGH HIGH SCHOOL COMBINED

Step 4
When discussing who the oppressed are, spend some time focusing specifically on differences, if any, that exist between junior high and high school. Ask: **What are the major forms of injustice at each type of school?** If you have more than two junior highers and two high schoolers, have them meet separately to develop lists of the injustices they think are most common at their grade levels. Then bring the groups together and have them share their lists. Note similarities and differences. Afterward, have the groups work together in coming up with a list of other forms of oppression and injustice in society.

Step 5
You might think that junior highers won't have as great an interest in, or ability to do anything about, fighting injustice. Think again. Given proper motivation, they can get very enthusiastic about doing something specific. What they might lack, however, is persistence and follow-through. To help with this, pair kids up (preferably one older kid with one younger one). Have them share one specific thing they each plan to do to fight injustice. Have them exchange phone numbers and promise to call each other at least one time to see if they've had a chance to do anything yet. If you don't think your kids will actually make phone calls, give them some opportunities to keep talking about this subject in future sessions. It would only take a minute or two. Add some type of incentive—give a reward (a small treat or some other special recognition) when they report back (as a pair) that they followed through on their individual commitments.

EXTRA CHALLENGE

Step 3
After discussing the definitions of justice and injustice, write on the board "Justice or Just Us?" Ask: **What do you suppose I mean by this question?** Help kids see that it's easy to cry for justice when we are the ones at a disadvantage; it's another thing altogether to cry for justice for others who are oppressed, especially when they are people we have a hard time identifying with. Then discuss some tough questions:

- **Why does God allow injustice?**
- **What are you willing to sacrifice in order to help others find justice?**
- **Is true justice possible in a sinful world?**
- **How would you respond to someone who says poor people bring trouble on themselves?**

Step 4
Don't just stop at coming up with ideas your whole group can get involved with; think about some things your group can get the entire church behind. Here are a few ideas to get your creative juices flowing:

- Organize a canned food drive.
- Sponsor a child through an organization like World Vision or Compassion International.
- Purchase Christmas gifts for needy children.
- Contact city officials and find out what your church might be able to do during a one-day workday—away from the church.
- Organize and publicize a "Single Parents' Day Off" in which single parents are encouraged to bring their kids to the church for free baby-sitting for a certain number of hours.

PLANNING CHECKLIST

Date Used:

Approx. Time

Step 1: Musical Chaos _____
o Small Group
o Large Group
o Mostly Guys
o Extra Fun
o Media
o Short Meeting Time
Things needed:

Step 2: A Need to Stand _____
o Extra Action
o Mostly Girls
o Mostly Guys
o Urban
Things needed:

Step 3: The Just . . . _____
o Large Group
o Heard It All Before
o Little Bible Background
o Extra Challenge
Things needed:

Step 4: What Can We Do? _____
o Media
o Urban
o Combined Junior High/High School
o Extra Challenge
Things needed:

Step 5: Even You . . . _____
o Small Group
o Little Bible Background
o Fellowship & Worship
o Mostly Girls
o Short Meeting Time
o Combined Junior High/High School
Things needed:

Step 6: Holy Wrap-Up _____
o Extra Action
o Heard It All Before
o Fellowship & Worship
o Extra Fun
Things needed:

Custom Curriculum Critique

Please take a moment to fill out this evaluation form, rip it out, fold it, tape it, and send it back to us. This will help us continue to customize products for you. Thanks!

1. Overall, please give this *Custom Curriculum* course (*What, Me Holy?*) a grade in terms of how well it worked for you. (A=excellent; B=above average; C=average; D=below average; F=failure) Circle one.

   A B C D F

2. Now assign a grade to each part of this curriculum that you used.

a. Upfront article	A	B	C	D	F	Didn't use
b. Publicity/Clip art	A	B	C	D	F	Didn't use
c. Repro Resource Sheets	A	B	C	D	F	Didn't use
d. Session 1	A	B	C	D	F	Didn't use
e. Session 2	A	B	C	D	F	Didn't use
f. Session 3	A	B	C	D	F	Didn't use
g. Session 4	A	B	C	D	F	Didn't use
h. Session 5	A	B	C	D	F	Didn't use

3. How helpful were the options?
   - ❑ Very helpful
   - ❑ Somewhat helpful
   - ❑ Not too helpful
   - ❑ Not at all helpful

4. Rate the amount of options:
   - ❑ Too many
   - ❑ About the right amount
   - ❑ Too few

5. Tell us how often you used each type of option (4=Always; 3=Sometimes; 2=Seldom; 1=Never)

	4	3	2	1
Extra Action	❑	❑	❑	❑
Combined Jr. High/High School	❑	❑	❑	❑
Urban	❑	❑	❑	❑
Small Group	❑	❑	❑	❑
Large Group	❑	❑	❑	❑
Extra Fun	❑	❑	❑	❑
Heard It All Before	❑	❑	❑	❑
Little Bible Background	❑	❑	❑	❑
Short Meeting Time	❑	❑	❑	❑
Fellowship and Worship	❑	❑	❑	❑
Mostly Guys	❑	❑	❑	❑
Mostly Girls	❑	❑	❑	❑
Media	❑	❑	❑	❑
Extra Challenge (High School only)	❑	❑	❑	❑
Sixth Grade (Jr. High only)	❑	❑	❑	❑

6. What did you like best about this course?

7. What suggestions do you have for improving *Custom Curriculum*?

8. Other topics you'd like to see covered in this series:

9. Are you?
❑ Full time paid youthworker
❑ Part time paid youthworker
❑ Volunteer youthworker

10. When did you use *Custom Curriculum*?
❑ Sunday School ❑ Small Group
❑ Youth Group ❑ Retreat
❑ Other ______________________________

11. What grades did you use it with? ____________

12. How many kids used the curriculum in an average week? ________

13. What's the approximate attendance of your entire Sunday school program (Nursery through Adult)? _______

14. If you would like information on other *Custom Curriculum* courses, or other youth products from David C. Cook, please fill out the following:

Name: ______________________________
Church Name: ______________________________
Address: ______________________________
____
Phone: (____) ______________________________

Thank you!